T0326242

Cambridge Elements

Elements in Corpus Linguistics
edited by
Susan Hunston
University of Birmingham

SOCIAL GROUP REPRESENTATION IN A DIACHRONIC NEWS CORPUS

Irene Elmerot
Stockholm University

CAMBRIDGE
UNIVERSITY PRESS

 CAMBRIDGE
UNIVERSITY PRESS

Shaftesbury Road, Cambridge CB2 8EA, United Kingdom

One Liberty Plaza, 20th Floor, New York, NY 10006, USA

477 Williamstown Road, Port Melbourne, VIC 3207, Australia

314–321, 3rd Floor, Plot 3, Splendor Forum, Jasola District Centre,
New Delhi – 110025, India

103 Penang Road, #05–06/07, Visioncrest Commercial, Singapore 238467

Cambridge University Press is part of Cambridge University Press & Assessment,
a department of the University of Cambridge.

We share the University's mission to contribute to society through the pursuit of
education, learning and research at the highest international levels of excellence.

www.cambridge.org
Information on this title: www.cambridge.org/9781009500166

DOI: 10.1017/9781009029063

First published 2025

A catalogue record for this publication is available from the British Library

ISBN 978-1-009-50016-6 Hardback
ISBN 978-1-009-01421-2 Paperback
ISSN 2632-8097 (online)
ISSN 2632-8089 (print)

Cambridge University Press & Assessment has no responsibility for the persistence
or accuracy of URLs for external or third-party internet websites referred to in this
publication and does not guarantee that any content on such websites is, or will
remain, accurate or appropriate.

Social Group Representation in a Diachronic News Corpus

Elements in Corpus Linguistics

DOI: 10.1017/9781009029063
First published online: January 2025

Irene Elmerot
Stockholm University

Author for correspondence: Irene Elmerot, irene.elmerot@slav.su.se

Abstract: Equality is a global factor of prosperity in democratic societies. In this Element, thirty years of newspapers and magazines form the basis of an intersectional study on how different social actors are described in Czechia. A bird's-eye perspective points to the news being very white male-oriented, but when scrutinising further, some results differ from previous studies, giving insights on linguistic othering and stratification that may be a threat to equality. The methodology can be used for most languages with a sufficient amount of digitised, annotated and available texts. Since more and more text is being gathered to form data sets large enough to answer any question one might have, this Element helps uncover why one should be careful about which conclusions to draw if the words put into the data are not adapted to the relevant register and context. This title is also available as Open Access on Cambridge Core.

This Element also has a video abstract: www.cambridge.org/EICL-Elmerot

Keywords: news discourse, sentiment in news, intersectional analysis, Czech language, corpus linguistics

ISBNs: 9781009500166 (HB), 9781009014212 (PB), 9781009029063 (OC)
ISSNs: 2632-8097 (online), 2632-8089 (print)

Contents

1 Introduction

Equality is a fundamental human right, as seen in the Universal Declaration of Human Rights that was adopted by a majority of the United Nations (UN) member countries in 1948. Although a few countries abstained from adopting it in 1948, and others did not join the UN until later, most countries have since promoted human rights in their governmental policies. This Element examines how different social groups are represented in the media and therefore whether or not they are indeed treated equally in texts read by a large portion of the adult population. The case in point is the Czech Republic, or Czechia, a country that emerged in 1993 from the dissolution of Czechoslovakia, that in turn had been through decades of different oppressive governments from 1938 to 1989. During these years, human rights were often violated in society, and in 1948, communist-led Czechoslovakia was one of the countries that abstained from signing the Universal Declaration of Human Rights (United Nations 1948).

Contributing to inequality is the human tendency to stratify people and things. Stratification involves arranging abstract or concrete things or individuals into different groups, as it helps us understand our world. However, 'othering', a negative consequence of stratification, not only divides people into different groups but also views those who are different from us in a less positive light. This Element will explore whether people from different social groups have been represented equally in Czech news press, or if and to what extent they have been stratified and othered.

In most of this Element there will be a bird's-eye view of general trends in the positivity and negativity used to represent the people in focus, but there will also be some close-reading discourse analyses in each section. Using the *Subjectivity Lexicon for Czech* (Veselovská and Bojar 2013), the co-occurrence of evaluative adjectives with nouns for different people in the data reveals the positivity and negativity associated with these people. This evaluation often contributes to the stratification and othering of the people in the data and is even sometimes found to be a recurring discourse. If, for instance, an Ethiopian person is described with an adjective such as 'hurt' and a Ukrainian person with 'fragile', rather than with adjectives such as 'wonderful' or 'honest', there may be negative discourse and linguistic othering towards these people and their country of origin. Such a discourse is then assumed to influence the receivers' perception of these individuals.

Many research areas outside of language and linguistics now use language and discourse to study various aspects of society. However, it is important to note that linguists need to play a crucial role in such studies. Linguists possess knowledge of the construction-related parts of speech and the fundamental building blocks of language. Linguistic knowledge is valuable for researching political and economic issues; however, the language in use has often been studied also by non-linguists. Some examples are Musílek and Katrňák (2015) on social class, and a popular science blog post by Malík and Pavlasová (2018) on that year's presidential election campaign in Czechia that used the same lexicon (or word list) as this Element. A similar lexicon was used by Loughran and McDonald (2011) to draw conclusions about the tone of financial texts. In the field of economics, some researchers (e.g. Ferguson-Cradler 2023) have identified the use of language analysis as a 'narrative turn'. However, they choose to highlight the black box operations of natural language processing (NLP) instead of using more transparent tools, such as those employed by corpus linguists. Many of those studies involve the creation of word lists or reference to such lists, which is an example of a basic but valuable linguistic research tool. As examples of where linguists have indeed worked on social issues, specifically concerning othering, there are several studies on the conflicts and war in Ukraine. These studies could have helped policymakers understand what was to come (e.g. Berrocal 2017; Fidler & Cvrček 2018 and the enlightening anthology edited by Knoblock 2020).

The main aim of this Element is to determine whether or not the social groups in focus, that is, groups defined by gender or occupation, are represented equally. To do so, the research questions are as follows: (a) which groups are more often positively or negatively evaluated? and (b) in which years in the dataset is that evaluation more frequent, that is, which changes can be seen over time for the different groups? A secondary methodological aim is to use the data presented in this Element to reveal limitations in a number of research resources. These resources are the classifications of the Subjectivity Lexicon (tested throughout this Element), the ISCO (International Standard Classification of Occupations) groups and their hierarchy (in Section 2) and the semantic categories (in Section 3).

This Element is an attempt to see what results may emerge if the data is approached almost purely quantitatively. In this introductory section, I will explain the relevant concepts, briefly address other subjectivity or sentiment analysis studies and explain the Czech background in particular as well as the dataset and tools. Sections 2 and 3 present the new analyses and are concluded by a discussion of the findings, advantages and limitations of the tools and methods used.

1.1 Othering and Stratification in the Data

Two of the tools used facilitate a stratification approach: the Subjectivity Lexicon for Czech establishes the categories 'positive', 'negative' or 'both' (see Section 1.3), and the ISCO list establishes ten groups of occupational titles (see Section 2.2). Combining these tools in analyses may reveal othering. Two examples would be if the nouns in an occupational group of lower socio-economic status are more consistently modified by negatively classified adjectives than the nouns in a group of higher status, or if some evaluative adjectives are only modifying women and not men, or vice versa.

Three principles underlie the research in this Element. The first principle is societal: we need to know and understand historical subjective representations to comprehend the reasons behind certain groups' positions in society today and the attitudes that led to them. Using this knowledge, we may avoid problematic stereotypes. The second is technological: recent research has shown that large language models (LLMs), now often used in different kinds of services such as chatbots, can create or reinforce othering when given certain prompts (e.g. Zhang et al. 2018; Delobelle & Berendt 2023; Viola 2023). It follows that texts underlying such LLMs need to be analysed so that future texts can become more equal from the outset, before potentially being used to train an LLM. The third principle is methodological: it is challenging to express emotions and sentiments, the topic of this Element, in language. Even seemingly positive words like 'happy' or 'delighted' may not accurately reflect a person's true emotions. As noted by several happiness scholars across non-linguistic disciplines, from Kanouse and Hanson (1972: 47) to Moreno-Ortiz et al. (2022: 10–11), individuals tend to conceal their positive emotions more than their negative ones. This phenomenon has been referred to as the 'negativity bias' or 'principle of negativity'. Without pre-empting the methodology section, I should clarify that I am not giving negative words more weight, as has sometimes been the case (e.g. Taboada et al. 2011), since the aims here are different.

The claim that recurring phrases and discourses leave an impression on us has a long history. In corpus-assisted discourse studies, the concept of prosody is often used for this (e.g. Tognini-Bonelli 2001). This concept is based on John Sinclair's concept of semantic prosody (Stubbs 2002: 66), suggesting that co-occurrences assist in creating a 'discourse prosody' – a mental connection similar in function to the sound patterns of intonation or poetry reading, a context where prosody is a more common term: 'Discourse prosodies express speaker attitude. If you say that something is *provided*, then this implies that you approve of it. Since they are evaluative, prosodies often express the speaker's reason for making the utterance, and therefore identify functional discourse units' (Stubbs 2002: 65).

In a Slavic context, Viktor Šklovskij (1914 [1973]) argued that once words become familiar, the less we notice them, precisely because we have internalised them. Roman Jakobson stated a similar thought, that linguistics is aimed at specifically revealing which parts of a 'universe' are given linguistic expression, and what this expression looks like (Jakobson 1960: 351). The idea that we are not aware of the biases the words in a text may have is reflected in more modern research, such as Hoey's (2015) theory on word priming, which suggests that only a corpus-based study can identify primings shared by most readers, of which they themselves might be unaware (15).

Researching linguistic othering in discourse is a significant feature in the research area of Critical Discourse Analysis (CDA). This Element is inspired by many such researchers who have also studied othering, for example Van Dijk (1988: 147), Fairclough (2015) and Wodak (2016: 3). However, the analyses in this Element begin with a bird's-eye perspective of the three decades that is wider than many CDA studies. They are also performed on a language much less studied than English, albeit with computational resources few other languages have.

1.2 The Case of Czech

1.2.1 Some Relevant Historical Background

Czechoslovakia, an independent country established in 1918 after the collapse of the Habsburg empire, was at first a country full of democratic hopes. The modern-day gender equality discussions, for example, have their main origin in the end of the nineteenth and the beginning of the twentieth centuries. The creation of a new country was a nationalistic project, and many women who wanted equal rights, or at least the right to vote, made those issues partly a nationalistic question (Feinberg 2022: 303) as a stance against the German-speaking empire. The idea that women are first and foremost mothers and wives was prevalent among both men and women (Frančíková 2017: 8, 19, 27, 118) but was also seen as an argument to make women's lives more equal when it came to the public sphere (Feinberg 2022: 305).

Explicit rights for women to be citizens of equal status with men, as well as all other residents irrespective of religion or origin, were eventually included in the first Czechoslovak constitution after World War I (Parlament Československé Republiky 1920: Article 106). This was a clear success for the women activists, after the previous Austrian Civil Code where the husband was the head of the family (Feinberg 2006b: 42–43), but the factual legal practice did not follow Article 106 to the word. The actual rights women eventually gained were mainly decided by the men of the commissions forwarding the law proposals to the parliament, which led to women still being bound by law to obey their husbands' word regarding the household (51). In the Czechoslovak Republic, the more radical activists eventually had to compromise with the more traditionalist women of their organisations, and arguments about family and nation prevailed during the interwar period (70). Despite Article 106 of the Constitution and the fact that the women turned this into a nationalistic cause more than a gender issue, they eventually did not succeed in much more detail than other nations in Europe during this time.

Furthermore, this new state, later called the First Republic of Czechoslovakia, only existed for twenty years. In 1938, the country was further disrupted following Nazi Germany's annexation of the Sudetenland in the north-west and Slovakia's subsequent declaration of independence. Following World War II, Czechoslovakia fell under Soviet influence, leading to a communist coup in 1948 – despite the democratic elections before this coup giving the communist party around a third of the seats in parliament. This regime, which on paper promoted equality for all, eventually imposed several totalitarian principles and central planning, and suppressed dissent. The newspaper language – as all public language – was consciously used to pressure the readers in the ideologically sanctioned direction, to the extent that the newspaper sections, such as sport, foreign affairs and finance, were constructed in more or less the same way (see e.g. the chapters by Hedin, Woldt and Gammelgaard in Kress 2012).

Another relevant note regarding both gender issues and occupational roles is that some women that supported the government of the Second Republic during the Nazi protectorate (1938–1945) defined the role women should have in society through the concept of 'equality in difference' (Feinberg 2006a: 100). This meant mainly accentuating women's role in the home, but at the same time reiterating the idea that housewives performed manual labour, namely something that should be seen to be as difficult and creative as labour outside the home (Feinberg 2006a: 104–105). In many ways, this idea seems to be kept through both the first (democratic) and the second (protectorate) republics, and then reformed again, when in 1948 the communist party assumed power (Feinberg 2006b: 206–207). Havelková notes (2017: 40–41) that large efforts were made during the 1948–1989 period to relieve women of household work, but she also claims that these efforts never changed the role of men, and thus never removed the burden on women. She also claims (302) that by the end of and after that period, the further measures taken (such as increased maternity leave) only reinforced the role of women as wives and mothers and made it more difficult for women to pursue a career. This is reiterated in Weiner's (2007) sociological study on the 1948–1989 period, adding that women did not receive the same wages even for the same work (27) – something that may be expected from an ideology that claims that all output should be equally distributed. Issues of equality that were discussed in the West during 1948–1989 were by the communist party considered 'bourgeois' and thus 'dangerous' (Fojtová 2016: 112) – equality should be discussed in the way the communist party decided. For example, women were said to 'help' with – not participate in – 'revolutionary tasks' (Oates-Indruchová 2016: 928).

The party's expropriation (Havelkova & Oates-Indruchová 2015: 10–11) of the equality discourse became an obstacle to future work – after 1989, very few wanted to use terms or theories that were deemed contaminated by the former regime (see for example Nyklová 2018). Cultural clashes often occurred when gender or feminist researchers from the West met with their colleagues in Czechoslovakia (1990–1993) or Czechia (after 1993). Some gender scholars, whether from the US or Europe, assumed their Czech colleagues would easily accept previous Western research, a phenomenon referred to as 'westsplaining'. These Americans and Europeans had to accept the fact that the concept of feminism carried with it certain negative connotations in this part of the world (Fojtová 2016: 113–114; Jusová 2016: 29–30).

However, opposition movements emerged, and in 1989, the communist regime eventually collapsed. Democratic presidential elections were held at the end of 1989, followed by parliamentary elections in 1990. The first president, Václav Havel, was a playwright and former dissident who wrote essays and plays about the totalitarian language used throughout this Communist society; how expressions that may for the uninitiated seem harmless are turned into despised expressions that make people want to turn their back on anything 'socialist'. This is a reason for this study to start in this point in time. The president of the Czech Republic maintains some legal power (see e.g. Kubát et al. 2021: 140), and Havel was succeeded by economists Klaus (2003–2013) and Zeman (2013–2023). The latter became famous outside the country when he held up a toy gun with the inscription 'For journalists' during a press conference. The prime minister during most of Zeman's years, Andrej Babiš, was often cited for promising to run the country like a business. The combination of Zeman and Babiš in the last decade of the analyses makes the time frame highly relevant for studies of representation in the news.[1]

1.2.2 The Czech Language

Czech is an inflectional, Slavonic language, with three genders (neuter, feminine and masculine), two numbers (singular and plural) and seven cases for nominal parts of speech (nominative, genitive, dative, accusative, vocative, locative and instrumental). This structure makes the word order more flexible than in languages such as English, since the cases explain which words go

---

[1] A contrast is Petr Pavel, president of Czechia since 2023. Pavel invited prominent women to a gathering in the presidential halls on 8 March 2024 and in his speech, he concluded that little has happened in gender equality over the past 100 years.

together within a clause or sentence. This also makes some research questions work better for studying the Czech language than they might for other languages. The features most relevant to this Element are the Czech language's ability to place an adjective far from its noun without losing the connection, to create feminine forms of nominal words and to easily turn a word into its opposite by adding the negating prefix 'ne-'. Following is an example, where the first adjective and its modified noun are underlined and the negation bold:

> *Napsala to včera agentura Reuters s odvoláním na **ne**jmenované tři současné a čtyři bývalé americké <u>činitele</u>.* '(News) Agency Reuters wrote this yesterday, citing three current and four former US [male] <u>officials</u>, all **an**onymous.'[2]

With the tools used, I intend to present methods that can be used for any language with the right resources. Furthermore, Czech is closely related to Polish, Slovak, Ukrainian and the other Slavonic languages, making this Element particularly useful for studies of and in those languages and countries.

1.2.3 Othering in the Czech Language

Othering in written Czech language has been studied by scholars such as Fidler (2016) who divided the results into three historic parts: just after the fall of communism in the end of 1989, before Czechia joined the European Union (EU) in 2004 and after the country's EU membership. She looked at collocations for the two words *cizinec* 'foreigner, stranger' and *mluvící* 'speaker(s)', and found, for example, a clear difference in the collocations of *cizinec* between the three periods. There was in her study, however, no enlarged discussion on the sentiments towards these strangers, providing another reason to analyse different 'others' in similar data.

The flexibility of the language also makes it possible to study othering by morphology, as in Thál and Elmerot (2022) who analysed the gendered endings given to transgender individuals in Czech online media and concluded that the clearest misgenderings were made deliberately. Using keymorph analysis (Fidler & Cvrček 2017) to study othering could be another option, but as yet there have been few attempts made for Czech (but see Fidler & Cvrček 2018 on the difference in agency between Russia and Ukraine). An important fact for this Element is that, unlike some other languages, for example Polish, the use of the feminine form of a normally masculine noun is unremarkable (Hodel et al. 2017: 395). When an occupation has a male and a female form, such as *malíř*, *malířka* 'male, female painter', the female suffix in Czech mainly tells the reader something of the painter's supposed gender self-identification.

---

[2] Mladá fronta DNES 21 April 2017. Czech National Corpus sentence ID: mf170421:17:2:2.

1.3 Tools and Data

1.3.1 The Subjectivity Lexicon for Czech

Not all languages are privileged to have any kind of subjectivity or sentiment lexicon available. For Czech, such a lexicon was published by Kateřina Veselovská (now Lesch) and Ondřej Bojar (2013). This lexicon remains the most comprehensive source of evaluative language available for Czech. Its components, aims and usage are described in detail by Veselovská (2013; 2017). Its origins lie in an American equivalent (Wilson et al. 2005) that has often been used in similar ways.

Lexicon-based sentiment analysis techniques are getting more and more popular (Benamara et al. 2017: 202; Bestvater & Monroe 2023) within NLP, both inside and outside linguistics proper. One example from outside linguistics is Asgari (2019), who used sentiment lexica from different languages to create a uniform model for sentiment analysis in different languages. He included the lexicon used in this Element (see Section 1.4) as one of the 'gold standard' tools to assess Bible translations and social media data (Asgari 2019: 171). A study within computational linguistics the same year comes from Zhao and Schütze (2019), who propose a 'universal approach for sentiment lexicon induction' (3514) by using a collection of similar lexica, including the Czech Subjectivity Lexicon. They do, however, conclude that several lexica needed manual adjustments or did not perform very well. Most of these and other sentiment lexica, as well as other tools, are based on modern-day reviews of entertainment websites and social media (Birjali *et al.* 2021). In contrast to the methodology employed in this Element, many of these studies on evaluation and sentiment use black box operations and are not very transparent.

The adjectives used in this Element are taken from the Subjectivity Lexicon for Czech and will be discussed further in the specific sections on occupations (Section 2.5) and gender (Section 3.3). Briefly, the adjectives, verbs and nouns in the Lexicon are classified into one of three 'subjective' categories: 'positive', 'negative' or 'both', depending on the subjective sentiment associated with them in Czech according to the researchers involved in that project. This is a research output that is useful if handled appropriately, and it is indeed a good start. Naturally, words alone do not cover the sentiment or tone of a whole text, which means that the results drawn from quantitative, semi-automated calculations must be compared to what was actually written. This is easily done with the material for this Element, since the corpus is a sub-corpus of the Czech National Corpus, freely accessible to all.[3]

---

[3] www.korpus.cz. Free registration is necessary to unlock all features, either individually or through an institution with Shibboleth access.

1.3.2 Problematic Issues with the Subjectivity Lexicon

In comparison to studies using all available adjectives surrounding certain nouns (in e.g. Islentyeva 2018, Zasina 2018 or Černá & Čech 2019), a problem for the Subjectivity Lexicon – as well as the semantic categories used in the gender section of this Element – is that its starting point was a translation of an equivalent lexicon for English. This translation included certain adjectives that should perhaps have been replaced by adjectives more frequently used in Czech text. A few examples are *maximalizovaný* from the English 'maximise', *korozní* from 'corrosion' and *zmocněný*, a translation of the verb 'empower', which only appear one single time each in the whole 1990–2018 Czech journalistic corpus. Another issue that had to be addressed early was the handling of negated adjectives. In Czech, both nominal and verbal word forms have an added prefix *ne-* in their negated form. The solution is that all negated adjectives in the dataset are classified as the opposite of their category in the Subjectivity Lexicon (e.g. the adjective *nesolidární* 'lacking solidarity' was classified as negative, because it is the negation of the positively classified *solidární* 'having solidarity'). A third issue is the dominance of multifunctional adjectives. The most frequent adjectives overall from the Subjectivity Lexicon are *velký* 'big, large', *dobrý* 'good', *rád* 'glad'[4] and *poslední* 'last'. The latter adjective has caused problems for previous studies on the language used in Czech newspapers (e.g. Křen 2017: 246–247). These four adjectives have sometimes been removed from the analyses that follow when they caused too much noise. Where that is the case, it is mentioned in the respective section. As Veselovská (2013; 2017) herself describes, there are more problematic issues, but most can be solved through qualitative reading of the actual source. More details are described in the following sections, but at the earliest stages of research design, a well-informed decision should be made about how to treat these kinds of issues.

1.3.3 Nouns with Adjectives

In this Element, evaluative adjectives that occur with specific sets of nouns are analysed as co-occurrences. The 753 adjectives of the Subjectivity Lexicon for Czech are classified into 'positive', 'negative' or 'both'. Their co-occurrences in news media with nouns indicating nationality and religion have been analysed in two previous studies (Elmerot 2021; 2022), as summarised here. In these previous studies, the nouns were taken from public statistical lists of

---

[4] In a construction with the modal verb *mít* 'have', it also means 'like', as in *To nemám ráda* 'I do not like that'. See Janda and Clancy (2006: 7); Tahal (2010: 151).

nationalities (Czech Statistical Office 2019) and state religion (United Nations Statistics Division 2020; Hackett & Grim 2012: 45–50;), as well as geographical and income-related classifications of countries (World Bank Group 2020). For Section 3, the female and male noun forms of these nationalities (e.g. 'Malaysian woman' or 'Portuguese woman') were extracted, as well as words for women, and their masculine equivalents, identified from the entry headed *člověk* 'human' from the most recent thesaurus for Czech (Klégr 2007). For Section 2, the main source of the nouns was the International Labour Organization's ISCO lists of occupational titles (see International Labour Organization 2022), with additional occupational nouns from both the previously mentioned thesaurus and a list of perceived prestige of different occupations in Czechia (Tuček 2019). The latter two formed a 'Non-ISCO' group.

For simplicity, two distinct terms will be used in this Element: co-occurrences and modifiers. Co-occurrences are the combinations of nouns and adjectives that go together in the same text, even if the adjectives might describe something in the context other than the people. In this Element, modifiers refer to the adjectives that appear just beside the nouns and, in these analyses, are prominent enough to affect the overall evaluation in a certain year or period. Modifiers may therefore include both attributive and predicative adjectives. The idea is thus to include both modifiers and co-occurrences, as both contribute to the discourse. For example, if 'nurse' is found one or seven words to either side of 'paranoid', both co-occurrences are classified as negative. However, the co-occurrences that are further apart, and thus not modifiers, are given less weight in the analyses. More details are found in the respective sections.

1.3.4 The Corpus

The co-occurrences of the previously mentioned nouns and adjectives were extracted into a dataset from the journalistic sub-corpus of the SYN (as in 'synchronic') series (release 8) of the Czech National Corpus, containing 4,499,370,372 (≈ 4.5 billion) tokens (running words, excluding punctuation) from approximately 200 titles. The SYN series are updated on a yearly basis, which facilitates repeating a study with newer material. This sub-corpus contains newspapers and magazines from 1990 to 2018, thus covering the period from the first democratic elections after the communist, Soviet-led regime to a new time of economic ups and downs, populism and migration-related debates. A multi-dimensional text study of genres based on the same corpus (Cvrček 2022) argues that these news outlets have gone through a shift from general to specific descriptions of reality, reducing the degree of cohesion and retreating from 'stated attitudes'. His study at the same time rejects theories about a tabloidisation of the news press during the same period as that discussed in this Element (32). The majority of the titles in the corpus are mainstream press, such as the dailies *Lidové noviny* and *Mladá Fronta DNES* and the magazine *Respekt*, but there are also a few titles that may be considered alternative press. One such is the *Parlamentní listy*, that began in print in 2003 and may have been a way for politicians to interact directly with their voters. Today it is better described as a nationalistic and socially conservative outlet of many re-used stories, with little journalism involved (Gregor & Mlejnková 2021; Štětka & Mihelj 2024: 188–189). Since it is a very popular outlet, it still merits its place in a corpus of what Czechs normally read. This journalistic corpus is thus an 'acceptably representative sample of a population of language users, a language variety, or a type of discourse' (Ädel 2020: 4).

1.3.5 The Constructed Dataset

The entire dataset constructed for this and the two previously mentioned studies has about 33 million observations or sampling points from the years 1990–2018, where each observation includes one adjective co-occurring with or modifying one noun in one issue of a certain newspaper or magazine. Table 1 illustrates the observations using two examples: the noun *Afričan* with the adjective *dobrý*, and the noun *Bulharka* with the adjective *zkušený*. The table shows the sentiment of the adjective, whether or not it is negated, and the frequency. When there are multiple co-occurrences of the same noun and adjective (as in the *afričan* example in Table 1, shown in the 'Fq' column), the variable 'adjusted frequency' (AdjFq column in Table 1) measures the average word distance between the nouns and adjectives for that text.[5] The idea is to measure the adjective's possible influence on the noun. In Table 1, *Afričan* 'African man' and *dobrý* 'good' co-occur several times in the same issue, but the fact that the adjusted frequency is lower than the raw frequency tells us that the adjective is not often a modifier to the noun. The second row, in contrast, shows *Bulharka* 'Bulgarian woman' and *zkušený* 'experienced' occurring once next to each other, giving an AdjFq of 1.

The adjusted frequency (**AdjFq**) is used instead of doing a search with pre- or post-modifying adjectives, based on proximity findings by Cvrček (2014). There may well be more than one word between the adjective and its modified noun and, in addition, adjectives in the near vicinity may be highly relevant for the analysis; see Table 2.

Example 1 in Table 2 does not contain a modifying adjective for *uklízečka*, but the noun is close to a modifier (*placené* 'paid') of another noun (*společnice*

---

[5] Calculated as AdjFq = SUM (fq × 1/distance).

Table 1 Variable examples from the data.

Sent	NegAdj	Noun	G	Adj	Fq	AdjFq
POS	A	afričan	M	dobrý	311	72.824117104206
POS	A	bulharka	F	zkušený	1	1.0000000

Legend

Sent = sentiment according to the Subjectivity Lexicon.

NegAdj = whether or not the adjective was negated in the corpus. The values are N = negated, A = not negated.

Noun = the denomination of a group.

G = gender of the noun in the corpus.

Adj = the adjective in its lemma[6] form.

Fq = absolute number of occurrences.

AdjFq = adjusted frequency (see the following discussion).

Table 2 Example (from the Czech National Corpus' application *Kontext*) of <u>adjectives</u> (underlined) and node **noun** forms (in bold) of *uklízečka* 'female cleaner'.

1 . . . učitelky hudby,	**uklízečky**	, <u>placené</u> společnice a komorné.
2 Jako <u>správná</u>	**uklízečka**	ví mnoho o životě rodiny a teď je ve hře . . .
3 . . . spolu s <u>mladičkou, sympatickou</u> a <u>věčně rozesmátou</u>	**uklízečkou**	Vanyou bydlí v domě.
4 Byla <u>ošklivá, zakomplexovaná</u> a pracovala jako	**uklízečka**	. Měla vztek na matku . . .

'female companion') of a similar category, in this case another low-paid occupation. If this had been a modifier included in the Subjectivity Lexicon, its classification there would have made this a classified co-occurrence. Example 2 does include an adjective included in the Subjectivity Lexicon, *správná* 'proper', modifier of the noun *uklízečka*. This is then classified as positive, according to the Lexicon's classification. Example 3 has three adjectives that all modify the noun: *mladičkou* 'very young', *sympatickou* 'nice' and

---

[6]   A lemma, plural lemmata, is the equivalent of a headword in a dictionary, encompassing all forms of one particular word. Stubbs (2002: 25) gives the following example: 'the lemma of the noun RABBIT is realized by the wordforms *rabbit, rabbits, rabbit's* and *rabbits*".

rozesmátou 'smiling'. All three are included in the dataset, with slightly different adjusted frequency values due to their different distances from their noun.
Example 4 has two adjectives (*ošklivá* 'ugly' and *zakomplexovaná* 'full of
complexes') modifying the unknown subject of the sentence. Here, the noun
uklízečka is a predicate nominative referring to the same subject, explaining
what she did for a living (*pracovala jako* 'worked as'). They are also included
and classified, but with different adjusted frequency values.

Before the quantitative analyses were performed, two more variables were
added. First, a variable called sentiment value was added, where a positive
classification from the Subjectivity Lexicon was turned into +1, a negative
classification to −1, and the occurrences where the adjectives were classified
as both became 0. This value was then multiplied with the adjusted frequency
for each observation, and the result is a variable called adjusted sentiment value:

$$\text{adjusted sentiment value} \ = \ \text{sentiment value} \ \times \ \text{adjusted frequency.}$$

The lower the adjusted sentiment value, the lower the impact on the results. This
adjusted sentiment value is then summed and shown per co-occurrence (of
adjective and noun) per year to reveal the difference between the positive and
negative classifications. In two previously published studies (Elmerot 2021;
2022) the calculations were based on the mean of this adjusted sentiment value
per year, meaning the results differ depending on how many published issues
each source (newspaper or magazine) had in the corpus each year. With the
summed value divided by the actual number of tokens in the corpus each year,
as in this Element, the positivity and negativity are recorded accurately no
matter how many issues were included. The results of these calculations give
an overall insight and can then be taken as a basis for a study that would focus on
modifying adjectives.

1.4 Nationalities Revisited

To briefly demonstrate the tools and methods and ensure intersectionality,
Figures 1 and 2 were created using data from two previous studies, calculated
in the same way as the rest of this Element. A brief overview of the data is
provided here, as the adjectives used were discussed in the two previous studies.
The research questions are as follows: which nationality groups are more
positively represented in the dataset, and what trends over time can be observed
regarding positivity or negativity?

The first study (Elmerot 2022) is on the representation of Arabs and Muslims
in the Czech media. In that study nouns are categorised into four groups: (I)
nationalities of Arab and Muslim-majority countries, (II) a reference or control

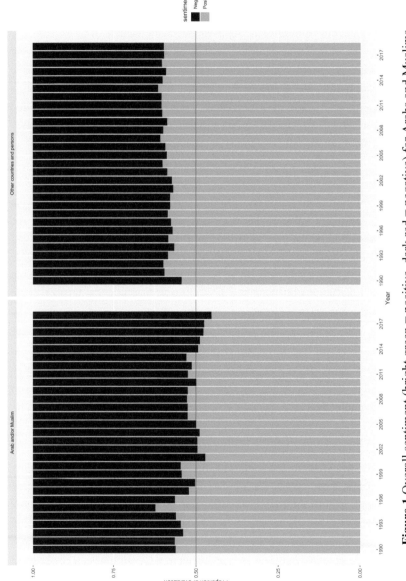

Figure 1 Overall sentiment (bright green = positive, dark red = negative) for Arabs and Muslims (countries and people) versus other countries and people.

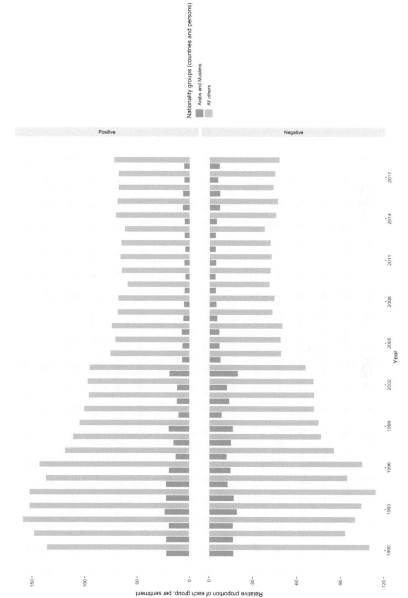

Figure 2 Frequency in the news with positive and negative co-occurrences, respectively, for Arabs and Muslims and their reference group.

group consisting of nouns referring to individuals with various nationalities and occupations, (III) names of the countries that have Arab- or Muslim-majority populations, (IV) a reference group of other countries. The control group consists of 2,619 nouns, while there are 99 nouns for Arabs and Muslim people (including country names). Figure 1 displays a graph equivalent to the previous study (Elmerot 2022: 129). The evaluation is presented in its entirety in Figure 1. If there were a perfect balance between positivity and negativity, the coloured bars would intersect at the horizontal line in the middle.

The findings here closely resemble those of the previous study (Elmerot 2022: 130–131). There is a peak in the positive representation of Arabs and Muslims in 1995, the year of the Dayton peace agreement, but in 1998, the negativity is more prominent. This becomes even more prominent in 2001, with only 2018 having more negatively classified co-occurrences. The only years where the positivity is more prominent for the Arabs and Muslims are 1990, which had a very small corpus, and 1995, due to the Dayton Agreement. This contrast in positivity indicates a distinct othering of this group, laying the foundation for negative discourses about them.

Then there is the question of frequency. Figure 2 displays the frequencies of positive (upper facet) and negative (lower facet) co-occurrences, normalised by the number of tokens in the entire journalistic sub-corpus per year. Naturally, the reference group has a larger proportion of the corpus than the group of Arabs and Muslims. However, there is a difference from the previous study: in 2003, there is a peak for Arabs and Muslims in both facets.

In 2003, the USA escalated their retaliation threats after the infamous 11 September 2001 attacks in New York, and there were many reasons for Iraq to be in the news. This further corroborates that study's arguments: Arabs and Muslims and especially their countries are represented as the enemy in the 'war on terror' – even in a small (NATO member) European country.

The other study (Elmerot 2021) focuses on countries categorised by their Gross National Income (GNI), using the World Bank categories of low, lower-middle, upper-middle and high gross national income (World Bank Group 2020). The aim was to determine if the hierarchy of these categories was reflected in the positivity and negativity classification of the Subjectivity Lexicon. Figure 3 represents the total sentiment equivalent of Figure 1 in the study (Elmerot 2021: 674).

The calculation shows that positivity increases with higher GNI, and the differences are more pronounced in the last two decades. Figure 4 displays the frequencies for GNI groups, relative to the actual number of tokens per year in the corpus. As before, nouns for both persons and countries are included.

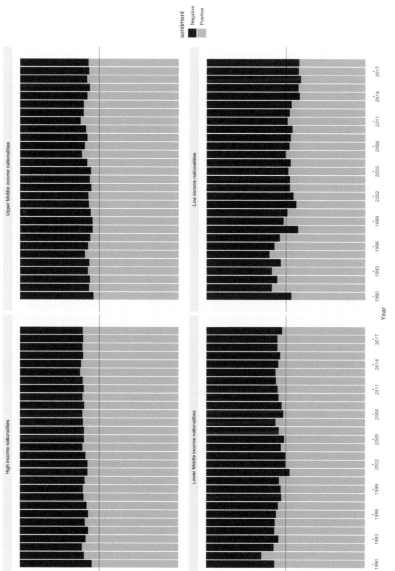

Figure 3 Overall sentiment (bright green = positive, dark red = negative) for the four income groups.

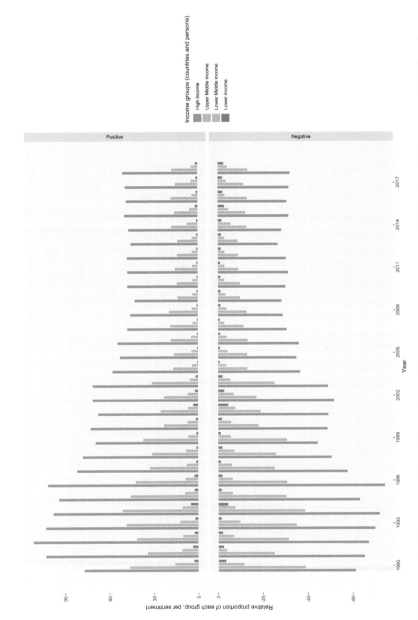

Figure 4 Frequency in the news with positive and negative co-occurrences, respectively, for all the nouns of the four income groups.

In this Czech news corpus, the frequency of co-occurrences with both positive and negative classifications consistently decreases from the high to the low national income groups. In addition, the launch of the 'war on terror', following the 11 September attacks in New York, seems to negatively affect the lowest income group in 2001, as seen in the long purple bar associated with that year. The negativity is mainly due to references to the low-income country of Afghanistan and its inhabitants.

1.4.1 Summary of the Othering and Stratification of Nationalities

During the Cold War, from 1948 to 1989, the Czechoslovak Republic was a part of the Soviet satellite countries. All countries behind the Iron Curtain were seen as sibling countries and neighbours. However, it now considers itself a part of the 'Western' world, together with the rest of the countries in the European Union (EU) and the North Atlantic Treaty Organisation (NATO). This change is reflected in the representation of other countries in the news media. The media uses similar amounts of positively classified adjectives to describe Czechs as it does for other high-income countries, according to the World Bank's classification. Generally, the adjectives in the Subjectivity Lexicon for Czech provide a clear stratification of the four income groups in that classification. The news press tends to use more negative adjectives to describe lower national income groups. When combined with these graphs, the qualitative analysis from previous studies shows that Arabs, Muslims, and particularly Afghans are the most distinct out group in the current millennium.

2 The Stratification of Occupations

There is a substantial body of research on how people in different forms of employment are represented in the news media, although this is more likely to come from the social sciences than the humanities. It is generally assumed that occupations can be divided according to status, and it has been argued that higher-status occupations are reported on more frequently and in more positive terms than lower-status occupations. Fairclough (2015: 79) observes that newspapers feature government ministers more frequently than the unemployed, and industrial managers and trade union officials more frequently than shop floor workers. However, he did not provide specific numerical data to support these claims. This section will determine whether there is equal representation across occupational groups in the data, focusing on both frequency and evaluation.

Research into the representation of occupations has been carried out in several countries. However, most seem to focus on the representations of teachers, often in comparison either between countries or with other occupations. In many places, teachers are represented as caring superhumans that face negative working conditions and, at least in the UK and Czechia, have a low status that sometimes reflects back on the teachers themselves and their performance. Female and male teachers also appear to be represented differently, with male teachers appearing less often in the news altogether, and often represented as lacking (Alhamdan et al. 2014; Elmerot 2017; Trčková 2018; Mockler 2022). The representation of different politicians, especially comparisons between female and male politicians, has also been the focus of many studies (e.g. Gidengil & Everitt 2003; Zasina 2018). Female politicians have been represented as aggressive, but also more often described using appearance-related adjectives. Zasina (2018; 2019) finds that the adjectives that define politicians of both genders are more often positively than negatively classified. These results are especially relevant for this Element as the data are similar, although Zasina looks at all adjectives modifying the relevant nouns, whereas this study focuses on adjectives included in the Subjectivity Lexicon for Czech. Studying the representation of less public and less qualified workers is harder, because they do not appear in the news as often as the teachers and similar socio-economic professions, but some studies exist. Migrant cleaners and housekeepers were shown to be perceived as 'poor, pitiful, vulnerable, and largely defenseless victims' (Nguyen & Do 2022) during the COVID-19 pandemic, and a more longitudinal study showed that construction and care workers are being mentioned less and less in the news press (Figenschou et al. 2021). Another study, using material that is also in the data for this Element, analysed the presence of class (Musílek & Katrňák 2015). When the authors searched their data for specific occupations and other groups of people (such as 'welfare recipients'), they found a 'strong tendency to symbolically divide society into distinct socio-economic groups', and that the groups with lesser income and status were objectified and being 'at risk of manipulation' (Musílek & Katrňák 2015: 408) in contrast to entrepreneurs and managers, who are described as successful, responsible and knowledgeable (406). The overall conclusion from these different studies is that researchers seem to favour teachers as an object of study, and that occupations of low to medium status, such as domestic workers, construction workers and care workers, are both less frequently and less positively represented than others. The negative representations, however, suggest powerlessness or victimhood rather than severe disapproval.

Occupational prestige refers to the value that an occupation holds in the eyes of the general public. Studies on occupational prestige have been conducted in various countries since the 1950s. Typically, prestige is evaluated on a per-occupation basis. For instance, a sample of the population in a country may be surveyed to determine the prestige of teachers or nurses. Occupations in the same socio-economic group or class as the researchers are often the focus, following the 'like me'-hypothesis formulated in the 1960s (Laumann 1965; a similar theory is 'Homophily in Social Networks' in McPherson et al. 2001), as seen in the analyses. Ulfsdotter Eriksson and Nordlander (2022) conducted a study examining occupational prestige for 30 different occupations based on the ranking by 3,375 individuals. The study aimed to identify possible differences between actual and perceived prestige. A part of their study is created similarly to the Czech prestige list;[7] see Section 2.2. The top three occupations on their list are physicians (medical doctors), lawyers, and professors (Ulfsdotter Eriksson & Nordlander 2022: 11), consistent with the Czech list. The authors conclude that their raters tended to favour occupations in the same prestige sphere as their own. Shifting the focus to Czechia, Drahokoupil (2015) reported that during the 2000s, many middle-class groups began to self-identify differently, often due to the low salaries paid to government officials of various kinds. This led to more research about this group by researchers who belong to it, as confirmed by Keller (2015). It thus seems that the 'like me'-hypothesis is not only valid for what prestige people assign occupations, but also for the occupations people write about, whether in scientific journals or newspapers. In other words, journalists may write about other occupations using the 'like-me' principle.

To summarise, most of the research on occupational stratification based on prestige has been qualitative rather than quantitative, and synchronic rather than diachronic. The few exceptions to this were mentioned previously. Even when quantitative, previous research has tended to focus on the representation of one or two occupations only. In addition, the impressionistic notion of 'higher' or 'lower' status, based on interviews, has not been verified by evidence.

The 708 occupations analysed in this Element were selected using both the International Labour Organization's standard list of occupations (Czech version, here referred to as ISCO) and a Czech 'prestige list' (Tuček 2019). The ISCO classifications are commonly used in the social sciences and have influenced regional lists, which have a similar breakdown of different groups. Examples include the Erikson–Goldthorpe–Portocarero classes scheme (EGP,[8] Erikson et al. 1979) and the European Socio-economic Classification (ESeC2). Katrňák (2012) found that these ISCO classifications are also valid for Czech society and adequately represent Czech socio-economic groups. Finally,

---

[7] A difference in their list, compared to the Czech, is that military and clergy occupations are absent from the Swedish list.

[8] Sometimes referred to only as the Goldthorpe Classes, or as the Comparative Study of Social Mobility in Industrial Nations, read more at www.encyclopedia.com/social-sciences/dictionaries-thesauruses-pictures-and-press-releases/goldthorpe-class-scheme. [Accessed 13 March 2024].

van Leeuwen et al.'s (2002a,b) augmented historical ISCO list is a useful theoretical tool for understanding representation and stratification. There, the original list has been expanded to include the concept of supervision, as they believe that the supervisory aspect of an occupation affects its socio-economic status. In this section, I will analyse the co-occurrences' sentiment and frequency in the news through these stratifying variables.

2.1 Research Questions and Aim

The primary aim of this section is to analyse whether people from different socio-economic groups are represented equally in the corpus. That means analysing how the groups of a lower socio-economic status are mentioned and evaluated compared to the groups of a higher status. If the 'like me'-hypothesis that individuals tend to associate with others who are similar to themselves is confirmed in this material, ISCO group 2, the one to which journalists belong, is expected to be the most prevalent. Following Fairclough (2015:79), it is hypothesised that the hierarchy of ISCO groups (explained in Section 2.2) will be more or less adhered to in terms of frequency of mention. The following questions will be addressed:

1. (a) How are the different ISCO group(s) positively and negatively evaluated, and (b) how frequently do they occur in the dataset?
2. How do the evaluative adjectives reflect occupational prestige or status within the ISCO labels 0–9?
3. Which changes over time can be seen for the different ISCO groups?

Some previous findings, such as the scarcity of mentions of elementary professions (ISCO 9) and the prevalence of references to managers (ISCO 1), are also expected to be found here and form a test for the robustness and generalisability of the current findings. The results per group are also analysed to determine the extent and manner in which they are affected by the Subjectivity Lexicon and the combination of occupations into ISCO groups.

2.2 ISCO and the Prestige List

In this section, I use the fourth version of the International Standard Classification of Occupations (ISCO, International Labour Organization 2004) published in 2008 as an externally verified stratification of occupations. The classifications have been published by the International Labour Organization, a United Nations agency. Its aims are threefold: to be used as a first option for reporting on comparable issues regarding work, as a template for national classification of occupations, and as a template for countries or regions that need to create such a classification.

Table 3 and the definitions that follow are an abbreviated version of the ISCO-08 EN Structure and definitions table (International Labour Organization 2008).[9] They present the overall titles and descriptions used for the classification groups used in the present study. The Czech titles are the official translations.[10]

The ISCO groups 1 and 2 could be said to belong to the upper middle classes; groups 3–7 constitute middle and 'upper lower' class occupation titles; groups 8 and 9 include occupations that require limited education and might be expected to attract a lower status. We can therefore derive three broad groupings from the ISCO groups. It is anticipated, following Fairclough (2011), that groups 1 and 2 will receive more mentions in the corpus and will be more evaluated overall, and that groups 3–7 will be less mentioned or evaluated.

To complement the ISCO groups for Czech society, another list, the Prestige list (*Prestiž povolání*), was also used to identify the status of occupational names. This list has been developed by sociologists at the Czech Academy of Sciences (Tuček 2019) and this section uses the nouns from the 2019 version. The list is designed to reflect public perceptions of occupations, and changes in those perceptions. According to Tuček, it was created by giving 1,024 respondents over the age of 15 a list of twenty-six occupations (see Table 8 with my translation into English), instructing them to select the occupation they value most and award it 99 points, then award 01 to the one they value least, and finally assign points from 02 to 98 for all the remaining occupations.[11] Physicians (*lékař*) have ranked highest throughout the years. In the survey from 2019, 45 per cent of the respondents awarded 99 points to the role of physician. The other occupations at the top of the list have also remained stable, as seen in Table 4. Tuček concludes that the prestige ranking shows little variability, except for the rise of the security forces (*voják* 'soldier' and *policista* 'police officer') and the decline of occupations related to politics and management (e.g. *novinář* 'journalist' and *ministr* 'minister').

---

[9] The full list can be downloaded from https://www.ilo.org/publications/international-standard-classification-occupations-2008-isco-08-structure.

[10] The whole list in Czech can be found on the Czech Statistical Office's website: https://csu.gov.cz/klasifikace_zamestnani_-cz_isco-

[11] My thanks to Milan Tuček for sending me the questions they posed in 2019 along with the results. The original question for the occupational prestige was *Na seznamu jsou uvedena některá povolání. Vyberte povolání, jehož si vážíte nejvíce a dejte mu 99 bodů. Pak vyberte takové, jehož si vážíte nejméně a obodujte je číslem 01. Poté postupujte odshora dolů a všem zbývajícím přiřaďte body od 02 do 98 podle osobního uvážení.*

Table 3 Classification codes with Czech and English titles.

ISCO 08 Code	Title CS	Title EN
1	Zákonodárci a řídící pracovníci	Managers
2	Specialisté	Professionals
3	Techničtí a odborní pracovníci	Technicians and Associate Professionals
4	Úředníci	Clerical Support Workers
5	Pracovníci ve službách a prodeji	Service and Sales Workers
6	Kvalifikovaní pracovníci v zemědělství, lesnictví a rybářství	Skilled Agricultural, Forestry and Fishery Workers
7	Řemeslníci a opraváři	Craft and Related Trades Workers
8	Obsluha strojů a zařízení, montéři	Plant and Machine Operators, and Assemblers
9	Pomocní a nekvalifikovaní pracovníci	Elementary Occupations
0	Zaměstnanci v ozbrojených silách	Armed Forces Occupations

Table 3 definitions:

1 Managers plan, direct, coordinate and evaluate the overall activities of enterprises, governments and other organisations.

2 Professionals increase the existing stock of knowledge; apply scientific or artistic concepts and theories; teach about the foregoing in a systematic manner; or engage in any combination of these activities.

3 Technicians and associate professionals perform technical and related tasks connected with research and the application of scientific or artistic concepts and operational methods, and government or business regulations.

4 Clerical support workers record, organise, store, compute and retrieve information, and perform a number of clerical duties in connection with money-handling operations, travel arrangements, requests for information, and appointments.

5 Service and sales workers provide personal and protective services related to travel, housekeeping, catering, personal care, or protection against fire and unlawful acts, or demonstrate and sell goods in wholesale or retail shops and similar establishments, as well as at stalls and on markets.

6 Skilled agricultural, forestry and fishery workers grow and harvest field or tree and shrub crops, gather wild fruits and plants, breed, tend or hunt animals, produce a variety of animal husbandry products; cultivate, conserve and exploit forests; breed or catch fish; and cultivate or gather other forms of aquatic life in order to provide food, shelter and income for themselves and their households.

7 Craft and related trades workers apply specific technical and practical knowledge and skills in the fields to construct and maintain buildings; form metal; erect metal structures; set machine tools or make, fit, maintain and repair machinery, equipment

or tools; carry out printing work; and produce or process foodstuffs, textiles and wooden, metal and other articles, including handicraft goods. The work is carried out by hand and by hand-powered and other tools.

8 Plant and machine operators, and assemblers operate and monitor industrial and agricultural machinery and equipment on the spot or by remote control; drive and operate trains, motor vehicles and mobile machinery and equipment; or assemble products from component parts according to strict specifications and procedures.

9 Elementary occupations involve the performance of simple and routine tasks which may require the use of hand-held tools and considerable physical effort.

0 Armed forces occupations include all jobs held by members of the armed forces. Members of the armed forces are those personnel who are currently serving in the armed forces, including auxiliary services.

However, there are also other occupations that have changed significantly in prestige, such as managers (*manažer*, down 8), ministers (*ministr*, down 7), as well as the three occupations programmers (*programátor*), mayors (*starosta*) and professional athletes (*profesionální sportovec*) that all have fallen five places in the prestige list. I will return to most of these in the analyses. (Note that two of the occupations in Table 4, 'secretary' and 'cleaner', have the female form as the norm, while the rest have the male form – including the teachers.)

2.3 Data Extraction from the Corpus

As noted previously, the corpus used in this study is the news and magazines sub-corpus of the Czech National Corpus. The texts extracted from the corpus included at least one instance of both (a) one or more of the 708 occupation names described in Section 2.2 and (b) one or more of the 773 adjectives from the Czech Subjectivity Lexicon. That resulted in 8.69 million observations.

Extracting occupation names for searches is challenging, as multi-word nouns from the original ISCO lists cannot be included; two examples are *Pomocní pracovníci v rostlinné výrobě* 'crop farm labourers' and *Řídící pracovníci v oblasti strategie a politiky organizací* 'policy and planning managers'. Therefore, the occupational titles, including the ones from the Prestige list, are reduced to one- or two-word nouns. It is then important to scrutinise all these nouns to ensure they are still occupational nouns and do not have ambiguous meanings. One example is the single-word noun *řidič* 'driver', which is too ambiguous to be included – it most often means car drivers in general, not as an occupation. Another example is *příslušník*, originating from, for example, the ISCO titles *Příslušník Hasičského záchranného sboru ČR* and *Rada – příslušník štábu*[12]. The single noun means a member, a person belonging

---

[12] Literally 'Member of the Czech Republic Fire Rescue Service' and 'Council – member of staff'. Included under 'Fighter, fire' and 'Agent, inquiry: police' in the English ISCO08 index.

Table 4 The 'Prestige list' (Tuček 2019) with ISCO groups and my translations, ranked as in 2019.

Profese	Occupation	2004	2007	2011	2013	2016	2019	ISCO
Lékař	Physician	1	1	1	1	1	1	2
Vědec	Scientist	2	2	2	2	2	2	2
Zdravotní sestra	Nurse	-	-	3	3	3	3	1,2
Učitel na vysoké škole	University/college teacher	3	3	4	4	4	4	2
Učitel na základní škole	Primary school teacher	4	4	5	5	5	5	2
Soudce	Judge	6	7	7	6	6	6	2
Projektant	Designer	7	6	6	8	7	7	2,3
Soukromý zemědělec	Private-sector farmer	10	8	9	7	9	8	6
Policista	police officer	20	13	11	10	10	9	5
Programátor	Programmer	5	5	8	9	8	10	2
Voják z povolání	Career soldier	22	21	17	16	12	11	0
Truhlář	Carpenter	16	14	12	11	13	12	7
Starosta	Mayor	8	9	14	13	11	13	–
Majitel malého obchodu	Small shop owner	15	16	15	12	15	14	–
Účetní	Accountant	14	15	10	14	14	15	3,2
Profesionální sportovec	Professional athlete	11	10	16	18	16	16	3
Manažer	Manager	9	11	13	15	17	17	1,2

Stavební dělník	Construction worker	-	-	18	17	19	18	7 (3)
Bankovní úředník	Bank clerk	18	20	19	19	20	19	4
Ministr	(Political) minister	13	17	24	24	18	20	–
Prodavač	Salesman	24	23	21	20	23	21	5
Novinář	Journalist	12	12	20	21	21	22	2
Sekretářka	(Female) secretary	23	24	23	22	24	23	4
Kněz	Priest	21	22	22	23	22	24	–
Uklízečka	(Female) cleaner	26	26	25	25	26	25	9
Poslanec	Member of parliament	25	25	26	26	25	26	–

to a group, and was therefore excluded from the dataset. *Majitel* 'proprietor, owner' was scrutinised and found to most often refer to a business owner of some sort, which was a reason to keep it in the dataset.

Another methodological problem turned out to be that many of the more practical occupations have become surnames, such as Taylor in English, Zimmermann in German or Carnicero in Spanish. The dataset only includes lower-case lemmata for all nouns, regardless of their original capitalisation, which requires closer scrutiny of the corpus itself. During the analysis in Section 2.5, a deeper assessment was conducted on the corpus to determine the number of prominent nouns in each group that are also names, to prevent skewing the overall results. No nouns that are also names have been removed, but the results are commented on in the analyses.

As seen in Table 5, the most frequent noun in the occupations dataset is *trenér* 'trainer, coach', and the synonym *kouč* is also present in the top ten. This is obviously the result of newspapers publishing daily sports sections, as well as lifestyle magazines in certain instances. I have kept them in the data for the sake

Table 5 The 20 most common occupational titles and their raw frequencies co-occurring with evaluative adjectives. The last column gives their rank in the corpus in general.

1	trenér	training instructor	ISCO 3	648,452	1
2	ředitel	director	ISCO 1	478,810	2
3	starosta	mayor	Non-ISCO	381,222	4
4	ministr	minister	Non-ISCO	377,130	5
5	policista	police officer	ISCO 5	320,893	3
6	lékař	doctor	ISCO 2	314,067	7
7	majitel	owner	Non-ISCO	313,205	6
8	kouč	coach	ISCO 2	294,027	9
9	herec	actor	ISCO 2	210,776	11
10	režisér	director	ISCO 2	195,186	13
11	hasič	fireman	ISCO 5	185,651	8
12	poslanec	MP	Non-ISCO	182,365	10
13	manažer	manager	ISCO 1	174,999	12
14	voják	soldier	ISCO 0	150,090	14
15	učitel	teacher	ISCO 2	146,399	15
16	novinář	journalist	ISCO 2	146,265	16
17	kapitán	captain	ISCO 3	136,351	17
18	sportovec	sportsman	ISCO 3	123,450	19
19	úředník	clerk	ISCO 4	115,691	18
20	zpěvák	singer	ISCO 2	100,900	20

of completeness, even if their ISCO groups need some extra close reading to discern if or when these nouns give a biased co-occurrence result. The individual occupation names comprising each ISCO group vary in how frequently they co-occur with evaluative adjectives, as seen in Table 5. The group of Public officials etc. has the closest span between their top three most frequent nouns: *majitel* 'proprietor, owner' (313,205 co-occurrences for the whole time span), *ministr* '(political) minister' (377,130) and *starosta* 'mayor' (381,222). This means that not only is the group the second most frequent in raw numbers, but the group also has several of the most frequent individual nouns of the whole occupations dataset. As a numerical comparison, Military workers, ISCO 0, has an extremely wide span between its top three, with 13,620; 42,082 and 150,090 co-occurrences, and Elementary workers, ISCO 9, has a more average span with 10,205; 30,124 and 51,528 co-occurrences in the top three. The values in Tables 5 and 6 will be repeated in the context of Figures 7–9, where the number of co-occurrences are related to the journalistic corpus from which they have been extracted.

Compared to their frequency in the corpus without evaluative adjectives, police officers (rank 5), the members of parliament (rank 12) and the firefighters (rank 11) are clearly mentioned evaluatively less often.

When one or more of all these nouns occurred at the same time as one or more of the adjectives in the Subjectivity Lexicon, that instance, or observation, was extracted from the corpus into the dataset by means of a script in the R programming language.[13] The other scripts include code for assembling, sorting and visualising the dataset once it has been extracted from the corpus. Adjusted frequency was used to measure word distance and to include both attributive and predicative modifications, but also occurrences that may form discourse prosodies (see Section 1). These instances are classified into positive and negative evaluation. For example, 'happy' + 'politician' is coded as positive and 'sad' + 'politician' is coded as negative. This does not necessarily imply approval or disapproval of the person mentioned but serves to show with what general sentiment the nouns and their groups are represented in the news.

2.4 A Bird's-Eye View of the Occupations Data

In this section, the first analysis includes finding the groups that are more frequently evaluated in the news. Then the evaluation itself is scrutinised to see which groups attract more or less positivity. The evaluation is subsequently analysed in relation to the groups' frequencies in the media. Finally, the actual nouns and adjectives behind the figures are analysed in more detail.

---

[13] This was done from inside the corpus server. Other scripts for this Element available at https://osf.io/xzpju/?view_only=cb0ee3c198134174b0440f59095743c7.

Table 6 Frequencies of the different occupational groups.

Occupational group (ISCO no. in brackets)	No. of occupational titles included	No. of occurrences	No. of employees (1993–2018)	Occurrences per occupational title	Occurrences per employee, rounded %
(Non-ISCO) Public officials etc.	10	1,416,699	NA	141,669.90	NA
(0) Armed Forces	22	240,103	815,800	10,913.77	29
(1) Managers	15	780,455	6,610,100	52,030.33	12
(2) Professionals	162	2,638,220	15,771,800	16,285.31	17
(3) Technicians and associate professionals	147	1,566,409	22,100,400	10,655.84	7
(4) Clerical support	35	242,589	11,412,800	6,931.11	2
(5) Service and sales	70	952,984	19,134,200	13,614.06	5
(6) Skilled agricultural, forestry and fishery	22	169,876	2,117,000	7,721.64	8
(7) Craft and related trades	137	409,340	24,253,400	2,987.88	2
(8) Plant and machine operators, and assemblers	58	158,584	17,863,000	2,734.21	<1
(9) Elementary occupations	30	113,015	7,791,400	3,767.17	<1

The most frequently occurring group is the Professionals (ISCO 2), as seen in Table 5, but this is partly because this group includes the largest number of occupational titles (162). When dividing the number of occurrences in the news by the number of people employed in that sector, the Public officials group is instead by far the most frequently mentioned, followed by Managers (ISCO 1), as seen in Table 6. In this table, we see the number of occupations mentioned and the number of their occurrences in the dataset, followed by the number of employees in each ISCO group according to the Czech Statistical Office (2020). Then the occurrences, or mentions, are divided first by the number of occupational titles and then by employees with that title.

If the 'like me'-hypothesis was verified in this material, then ISCO group 2 should be the most commonly occurring. According to Fairclough's theory on the frequency of mentions (see the introduction to Section 2), the hierarchy of ISCO groups should be more or less followed, with the lower numbers (1–3) being the most frequent and the higher numbers (7–9) being the least frequent.

Table 6 suggests that the frequency of mentions in the news corpus does not correlate with the ISCO classification; thus, it is not the case that the higher socio-economic occupations are mentioned more frequently than the others. It is the case, however, that both the military and the agricultural, forestry and fishery group occur more frequently than a simple correlation between ISCO rank and number of employees would predict. It should be noted that Service and Sales workers (ISCO 5) have more mentions per title than the Technicians and associated professionals (ISCO 3). As predicted, however, ISCO groups 7–9 are the least frequently co-occurring in the media, but of those, Elementary occupations (ISCO 9) have the highest frequency rate per title, followed by workers in Craft and related trades (ISCO 7).

Compared, instead, to the actual number of employees in each group per year, the ranking is slightly different. ISCO group 0, military staff, would then be the most over-represented group during the 2000s – much more frequently evaluated in the news than employed in the country. This is explained by reports on military actions in other countries, which increase the number of occurrences. In ISCO groups 2 and 3, the correlation between number of occurrences in the dataset and the number of employees over time is also comparatively high. Another group that stands out in the 'Occurrences per employee, rounded %' ranking in Table 6, after the military, is the Skilled agricultural, forestry and fishery workers, ISCO 6. They probably make up such a high percentage of the occurrences because there are plenty of self-employed farmers alongside hobby fishermen and hunters that are not included in the statistics of employees. This group also has a very low correlation between occurrences in the dataset and number of employees.[14] Groupwise and for the entire period as a whole, it thus seems the journalists follow the 'like-me' principle to a certain extent, writing more about the professions in group 2, where they themselves belong, along with a few of the other groups.

2.4.1 Overall Evaluation

Figures 5–6 in this section are comparisons of only the positive and negative classifications to see which is dominant within the evaluated co-occurrences. Adjectives classified as both positive and negative, thus rendering a 0 as the variable value, are excluded from these figures. The sum of the absolute numbers for the two classifications per year are displayed using contrasting colours, bright green for positively, and dark red for negatively evaluated co-occurrences. If a group had an equal amount of positively and negatively evaluated co-occurrences, the green and red would meet at the black horizontal line.

To determine the most negatively represented occupational groups in total, Figure 5 displays the proportion of positive and negative modifying adjectives used for each group during the entire period. The x-axis indicates the ISCO group, and the y-axis indicates the proportion of evaluation. Figure 5 is sorted by the total amount of negative classification.

There are indeed clear differences between the groups in Figure 5, and there is neither a direct nor inverse relationship between the Subjectivity Lexicon's evaluation and the hierarchy of ISCO groups 1 to 9. Managers (ISCO 1), Professionals (ISCO 2)[15] and Technicians and associated professionals (ISCO 3) do have a similar overall amount of positivity, but Craft and related trades (ISCO 7) have an overall evaluation that is more similar to ISCO groups 1–3 than to groups 8 or 9. In comparison to ISCO groups 7 and 9 (Craft and related trades and Elementary occupations), Service and sales (ISCO 5) receives more negative evaluations. Additionally, in one year, the Service and sales group received more negativity than positivity, although the corpus for that year was rather small.

To show possible changes over time, the proportions per individual year are calculated. The results are presented in Figure 6.

Only one group, Plant & machine operators with assemblers (ISCO 8), received more negative than positive classification for more than one year. All other groups received more positive than negative classification over time, except for Service and sales (ISCO 5), where negativity outweighed positivity in 1994. The non-socioeconomic groups Military (ISCO 0) and Public officials (non-ISCO)

---

[14] Using Spearman's correlation (scale −1 to 1) on each ISCO group per year, the Professionals (2) received 0.642 and the Technicians etc. (3) received 0.727, while the Agricultural etc. group (6) got −0.737.

[15] Or *Specialists*, as they are called in Czech.

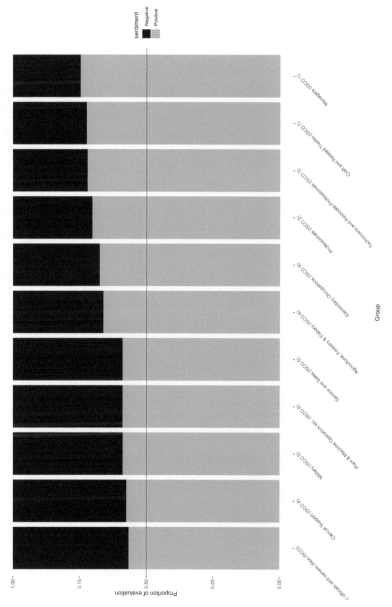

Figure 5 Proportion of negativity and positivity per occupational group for the whole period.

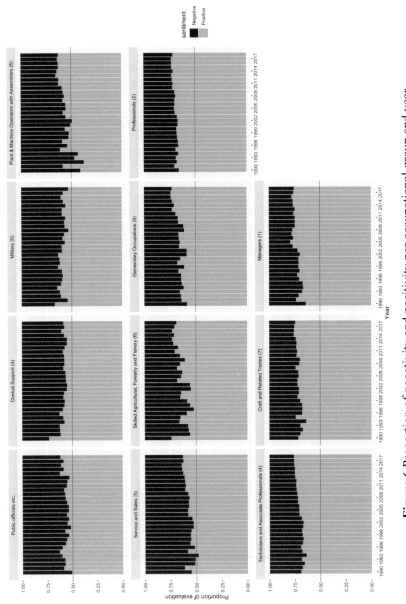

Figure 6 Proportion of negativity and positivity per occupational group and year.

appear similar to the Clerical Support (ISCO 4) and Service and sales (ISCO 5) groups respectively. ISCO 0 and ISCO 4 exhibit higher positivity at the beginning of the timeline compared to the end, while the other groups show the opposite trend. This order may be partly explained by the theory of supervision as a factor (van Leeuwen et al. 2002a: 52–53). The group with the most negatively classified co-occurrences for the entire period consists of occupations taken from the prestige list that belong to public officials or company owners – people to whom supervisors report, rather than the supervisors themselves. Following these are groups that are subject to some level of supervision, including military staff, clerical support workers and machine operators. The co-occurrences with the most positive classification throughout the entire period are found in groups where individuals may supervise others, such as managers and other types of specialists.

Figures 5 and 6 demonstrate that there is no precise correlation between socio-economic status and the extent of positive evaluation. An alternative grouping that better follows the data for this section is shown in figures 7–9. There, similar professions are grouped based on their frequency of mention and proportion of positive and negative ratings. For further analysis, three groups have been identified:

Lower: Clerical support (ISCO 4), Agricultural, forestry & fishery (ISCO 6), Plant & Machine Operators etc. (ISCO 8) and Elementary Occupations (ISCO 9).

Middle: Military (ISCO 0), Managers (ISCO 1), Service and sales (ISCO 5) and Craft and related trades (ISCO 7).

Higher: Public officials and owners (Non-ISCO), Professionals (ISCO 2) and Technicians and Associate Professionals (ISCO 3).

Figures 7–9 visually represent the evaluation of co-occurrences and their frequency relative to the total number of tokens in the original corpus. The *y*-axes of the charts represent a value obtained from twice the summed adjusted sentiment value, divided by the number of tokens per year. This is because each newspaper or magazine is published with a different number of issues each year. Figures 7–9 show the number of mentions for each occupational group within the groupings, represented by the length of the bars. The figures also display the normalised distribution of positive and negative evaluations, represented by the proportion of each bar above or below the central horizontal line. The scales differ between the positive and negative facets of the figures due to variations in the strength and frequency of positivity and negativity for different occupations. Figure 9 shows that the Clerical support group (4) has the longest bars in most years, indicating that there are more evaluated nouns in the news from this group than from the other groups in the same graph. Additionally, Elementary

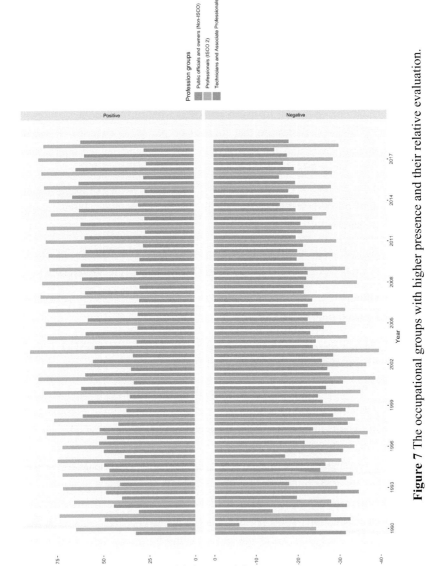

Figure 7 The occupational groups with higher presence and their relative evaluation. Y-axis numbers are relativised by the total number of corpus tokens.

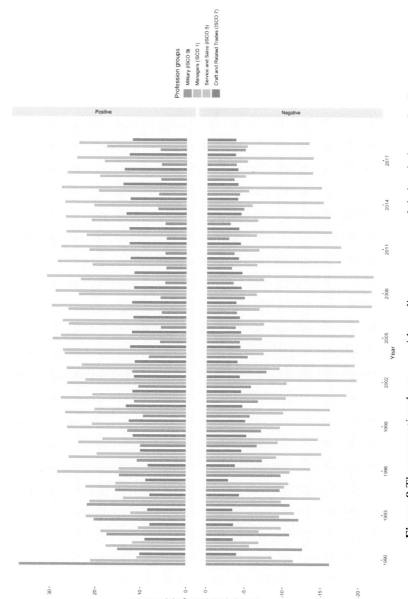

Figure 8 The occupational groups with medium presence and their relative evaluation. Y-axis numbers are relativised by the total number of corpus tokens.

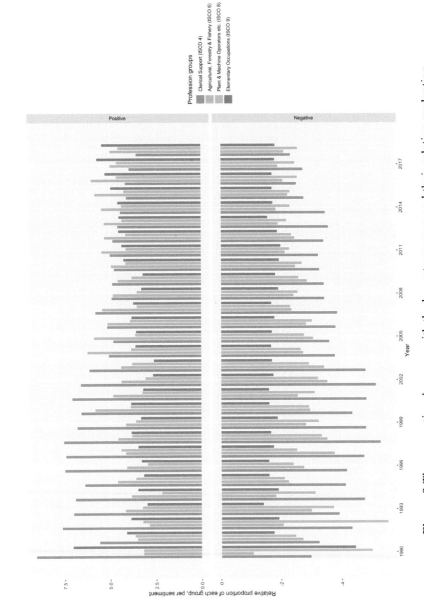

Figure 9 The occupational groups with the lowest presence and their relative evaluation. Y-axis numbers are relativised by the total number of corpus tokens.

occupations (9) often have the fewest mentions in both facets, but on the right-hand side, in the last two years, they have more positive co-occurrences in the news than any other group in this facet.

As previous research shows, the Professionals or Specialists (ISCO 2) – including occupations such as journalists, physicians, actors, judges, and singers – is mentioned more frequently than other groups. This is true for all years in positive co-occurrences and for most years in negative co-occurrences. The coefficient of variation, which is a relative measure of dispersion, is a useful tool for validating the results presented here. It is calculated by dividing the standard deviation by the mean of the relative sentiment value for each group. The results show that the Professionals (2) are the most stable group over time. Notably, the non-ISCO group, mainly composed of politicians, has the highest normalised number of negative evaluations, as demonstrated by the longest negativity bar in Figure 7. Despite this negativity score (−40), there is also a high positivity score (+52), which means they get an overall positive evaluation.

Figure 8 shows that the Service and sales group (ISCO 5) has positive *y*-axis numbers similar to those of the Managers group (1), while the negative *y*-axis numbers are close to those of Technicians, etc. (3) from figure 7. The Military group (0) and the Craft and related trades (ISCO 7) are most often the least occurring in this graph. At face value, the Military group appears more frequently at the beginning of the timeline, even when their numbers are relativised by the actual number of tokens in the corpus. However, soldiers are often featured in news stories related to other countries. Closer examination of the corpus reveals that prior to 2004, there were wars in Yugoslavia and debates about the Czech(oslovak) Republic(s) sending troops there. There were also debates focused on military issues before Czechia joined NATO in 1999. After 2004, there are more stories about older battles and military events. References to the extremely popular novel *The Good Soldier Švejk* are another reason for the high frequency of the occupation name 'soldier'.

Figure 9 illustrates that towards the end of the analysed timeline, these four groups exhibit similar values. However, Clerical Support (ISCO 4) has significantly more positive co-occurrences at the beginning of the timeline, and the Elementary Occupations (9) receive more positive co-occurrences towards the end. The Skilled agricultural, forestry and fishery workers (6) are evaluated the most in the middle part of the time period for both facets. The Plant and machine operators (8) and Elementary occupations (9) show similar levels of positive evaluation, with their bars often approximately equal in height. However, the Elementary occupations have a longer positivity bar and there are slightly longer negative bars for the Plant and machine operators.

2.4.2 Results of the Overall Evaluation

When studying frequency of evaluation in the news, it seems the previous research which collapses the ISCO groups into different overarching groups does not hold. Katrňák (2012) used a minimum of three (manual workers, non-manual workers and farm workers) or five groups (non-skilled, skilled and farm workers, as well as white collar and 'petite bourgeoisie') (683, compiled from Erikson and Goldthorpe 1992: 39), whereas we observe a different grouping here. The Clerical support workers (ISCO 4) cannot, for example, be grouped with manual workers, whereas some occupational titles in the Service and sales workers could be included in a broader group of non-manual workers. The theory on supervision taken from the HISCO classifications (van Leeuwen et al. 2002b) may provide a better rationale for the frequency of evaluation in the media: the groups that receive the most media attention and evaluation are Public officials etc., Professionals, and Technicians on a higher level, who are typically in supervisory roles.

Another reason could be service to and contact with other people. The middle group includes managers, who also supervise but may not always be appreciated, as well as the police and military, who supervise and give orders to the general public. All these professions involve close contact with the public, and the police at least have a role of serving the general public (Zákon č. 273/2008 Sb.).[16] While the supervision theory does not provide an explanation for why Craft and related trades (7) fall into this middle group, the service theory may offer some insight. It is important to note, however, that the frequent appearance of both surnames and famous deceased painters in this group may be the reason for its frequent media coverage. The media co-occurrence groups at the lowest level do not include occupations where supervision is an obvious part of their occupation, and they may often work far from other people. A combination of the theory of supervision with a theory about occupations serving others may thus be an important factor for a group to be more frequently mentioned with evaluating adjectives in the media.

2.5 Adjectives and Noun as Co-occurrences – Analyses of the Eleven Occupational Groups

Having undertaken the initial analyses, this section includes more detailed, interpretative studies of specific occupations and their evaluative prominence – this is often based on the most frequent evaluation or noun, but there is also discussion of some surprisingly frequent instances. The analysis tool is the co-occurrence of the prominent nouns and adjectives in each of the occupational groups. These analyses

---

[16] The Czech law clearly states this: *Policie slouží veřejnosti.* 'The police serve the general public.'

not only reveal some of the discourses around these occupations, but also highlight the limitations of using predefined datasets like the Subjectivity Lexicon and ISCO groups. Large parts of the analyses will thus point more to the importance of understanding the data used than to any binary sentiment of the groups.

The 'Higher', 'Middle' and 'Lower' groups created (see Figures 7–9) are the basis for the order of the groups that follow. The analyses include both the co-occurrences in general and the actual modifiers. The most influential (both evaluated and frequent) nouns or adjectives, that is, the ones having the largest impact on the graphs due to their high frequency, are scrutinised to determine their impact on the results.

2.5.1 The Higher Groups: Public Officials etc., ISCO 2 and ISCO 3

The Public officials, etc. group consists of ten titles, such as 'mayor', 'minister', 'priest' and 'ambassador', plus the non–public official nouns *majitel* 'proprietor, owner' and *stavebník* 'builder, constructor, developer'.[17] The Professionals group, ISCO 2, comprises the widest range of occupations, from physicians and nurses of various kinds to journalists, actors and teachers. Since journalists are included, the group's sheer frequency may be seen as a verification of the 'like me-hypothesis', that journalists mainly write about people in the same socio-economic group. The ISCO 3 group, Technicians and Associate Professionals, is in this dataset – despite its name – dominated by sports-related occupations from 1993 onwards. Additionally, it is one of the most positively evaluated groups in Figure 5.

In this Higher frequency section, the evaluative adjectives often do not evaluate the occupations themselves. In certain cases, they may instead assist in creating a discourse prosody (Stubbs 2002: 65) – an evaluative discourse unit. A clear example of this is the adjective *předchozí* 'precedent'. In more recent years, this adjective has a rather high co-occurrence with *majitel* 'owner', whereas in the 1990s, that noun tended to co-occur with *cenný* 'registered' or with *ochranný* 'protective, safety', mainly due to the bigrams *cenný papír* 'security, financial instrument' and *ochranná známka* 'trademark'. This indicates the significance of these new concepts in post-communist government discourse, as discussed in newspapers at the time. Another example of evaluative prosody is the noun *lékař* 'physician', with frequent co-occurrences in the top five negative evaluations, largely due to its association with the adjectives *nemocný* 'sick' and *zraněný* 'hurt'. However, the doctors themselves are frequently described as both *neschopný* 'incompetent' and *schopný* 'competent', with the former being one of the few negated adjectives in the top list.

---

[17] The latter two are a part of this group because they are in the Prestige list but not necessarily employed, as in the other occupational groups.

A previous study on the frequency of certain occupations in the Norwegian media found that construction workers and 'caring' occupations were described less frequently (Figenschou et al. 2021: 84). In this dataset, the only construction-related occupation that is clearly declining in frequency is *stavebník* from this group, which refers to builders, constructors and developers. The same phenomenon cannot, however, be seen for any kind of nurse in this dataset (there are four in total: *sestra, zdravotní sestra, vrchní sestra* and *staniční sestra*, in order of relative frequency). When their absolute frequency is normalised by the tokens in the corpus each year, their presence remains stable over time.

The evaluative development of journalists should be examined, since journalist is one of the nouns in the Prestige list that have experienced a decline in popularity in 2004–2019 (see Table 4). The dataset does not reflect the loss of prestige mentioned, except for 2018, where there is a sudden increase in negative co-occurrences for both male and female journalists, indicated by the negative adjective *zabitý* 'murdered', which this year co-occurred with journalists more frequently than any other year. This was due to the murders of two journalists in the neighbouring country of Slovakia and of a journalist at an embassy in Turkey. These incidents caused a stir in several European countries. Again, this shows that using pre-classified variables makes the need for close reading very important, as the journalist is described as having undergone a negative event, rather than behaving negatively.

Some examples of peculiarities indicating the relevance of close reading have been mentioned, but others may also be relevant for the design of future research. Among the top five most frequent positive co-occurrences in this Higher group, two are used with female nouns: *sestra* 'nurse' and *učitelka* 'teacher'. However, the most frequent, positively classified adjective for the latter noun is *základní* 'basic', which refers to primary or elementary school. The categorisation of adjectives is another peculiarity: *sociální* 'social' is categorised as a positive adjective, which leads to some problematic positive classifications. One example is the phrase *ministr(yně) práce a sociálních věcí* '(female/male) minister of work and social affairs'. *Sociální* is the most influential positive adjective in 1995, and the strongest driving force of the overall positivity throughout the whole timespan. Another positive adjective that also dominates in more recent years is *nezávislý* 'independent'. This is partly used about mayors who are not affiliated with a specific political party. However, since 2004 Czechia has had a political party called *Starostové a nezávislí* 'Mayors and Independents',[18] which has also created some bias in this dataset. The negative categorisations present a similar issue, as the adjective *stínový*

---

[18] The party has been in the European Parliament since 2009, the Czech Chamber of Deputies since 2010 and the Senate since 2012.

'shadowy' consistently appears alongside the most frequent nouns *ministr/ ministryně* 'male/female minister' throughout the entire time span, rarely describing any other group. This can be explained by the existence of a 'shadow cabinet' of ministers. The masculine form is one of the most prominent negative co-occurrences in both 2001 and 2013, with female ministers ranking 5th in 2001 after the formation of a special shadow government of women (see Section 3) and 13th in 2013.[19]

One of the groups, ISCO 3, is here dominated by sports, which is a large part of news media. The co-occurrences here most often represent the emotions of the occupation, rather than the evaluation. The noun *kouč* 'trainer, coach' appears in the top five with both negatively and positively classified co-occurrences. This noun appears more often in the negative co-occurrences, starting in 1998, and for four years only with the adjective *poražený* 'defeated'. In more recent years, the emotions behind these defeats have become more apparent, as the adjective *zklamaný* 'disappointed' is highly frequent among the negative co-occurrences. Among the positive co-occurrences, the noun appears in the top every year since 1999; in the top five only with the adjective *zkušený* 'experienced, skilled'.

The analyses also point to relevant results for writing about professions in a balanced or equal manner. When examining which adjectives most commonly modify the teacher nouns (not just co-occur with them), there are some differences between genders. The teacher nouns in masculine form are more frequently modified by the adjective *kvalifikovaný* 'qualified', which is the fourth most common adjective for them after the multifunctional *základní* 'basic', *dobrý* 'good' and *velký* 'big/great'. In feminine form, teacher nouns are often modified by *zkušený* 'experienced, skilled' (fifth most common modifier for both genders), but even more commonly, they are described as *hodný* 'nice, kind' (see Section 3.3.3). In contrast to previous research on teachers, the two adjectives in the Subjectivity Lexicon that may be translated as 'caring', *laskavý* and *starostlivý*, do not rank among the top fifty most frequent modifiers. *Laskavý* is present in the top 100 most frequent modifiers (at position 25 for female teachers and 66 for male teachers), but *starostlivý* is less frequent. Another adjective found in previous research on teachers is 'honest'. In this dataset, both *čestný* and *poctivý* 'honest' are used less frequently than 'caring' in reference to female teachers, but more frequently in reference to male teachers. *Čestný* is never used in its negated form, and *nepoctivý* 'dishonest' only once in the whole period, in the near vicinity of nouns referring to male teachers.

---

[19] This adjective is more or less only used about politics. If a flower would need a shad(ow)y place, the adjective used is *stinný*.

It is challenging to summarise these three groups, given the extensive scope of their representation within the dataset. A significant proportion of these occupations are perceived as supervisory, and the majority of them involve providing services to others. This may be a contributing factor to the high level of positivity associated with these roles, despite the prevalence of negative associations, such as those related to illness and mortality, in occupations within the care sector. A closer examination of the individual co-occurrences reveals the limitations of using a sentiment lexicon. In some instances, the 'positive' adjectives are descriptive rather than evaluative, as in the denotations 'qualified teacher' or 'elementary school teacher'. In other cases, such as 'journalist' and to a certain extent 'physicians', the negative adjectives used do not reflect an evaluation of members of the profession. This illustrates that a quantitative study alone cannot provide an accurate representation of an evaluative attitude, but it can serve as a valuable foundation for sentiment analysis.

2.5.2 The Middle Groups: ISCO 0, ISCO 1, ISCO 5 and ISCO 7

ISCO 0 is slightly different from the others, in that all professions are military. For this dataset, only the ones not present in other categories were included, and the two most frequent nouns are *voják* 'soldier' and *generál* 'general'. ISCO 1 comprises in this dataset fifteen different managerial nouns, but only three of them, *ředitel* 'director, head (of something)', *manažer(ka)*[20] 'manager' and *inženýr* 'engineer' (also an academic title, Master of Science) are mentioned frequently enough to make it into the top ten of the most evaluated and frequent co-occurrences per year. ISCO 5 has one dominant noun, *policista* 'police officer' with 34 per cent of the co-occurrences, followed by *hasič* 'firefighter' with 19 per cent and *strážník* with 11 per cent. Some years, the noun *strážce* 'guard' also is quite frequent. The noun with a third position in the dataset, *strážník* 'constable, warden', is sometimes close to being a synonym for a police officer.[21] These are represented as dangerous occupations, which is why this ISCO group is distinctive: it is one of the few to have more negative than positive evaluations in at least one year, and the negative evaluations have been as high as the positive for several years, as shown in Figure 5. Finally, ISCO 7, a group of Craft and Related Trades occupations, is dominated by the noun

---

[20] The feminine word form only made it into the top ten in the negative classified co-occurrences, with the adjective *krizový* 'crisis-', in 2017 and 2018.

[21] They are indeed similar, although *strážník* is in part more informal, and in part used more specifically for members of the city police force, whereas *policista* is more general. One way to study the differences in the usage is to use the *Word at a Glance* application at www.korpus.cz/slovo-v-kostce which shows their usage in both written (fiction and non-fiction) and spoken corpora.

malíř, which can be translated as 'painter' or 'artist', but may also refer to a 'decorator' or 'house painter'. Therefore, it is a broad term that encompasses both blue-collar workers and renowned artists such as Toyen, the Czech painter whose paintings sell for millions of both Czech crowns and British pounds. This scope explains why it has more than twice the number of occurrences compared to the second and third most frequent nouns in this group, *kovář* '(black)smith' (four out of six occurrences are surnames) and *krejčí* 'tailor' (almost nine out of ten are surnames). The fact that many of the nouns in this group are surnames again highlights the importance of closer scrutiny when using methods that cannot distinguish them. The analyses that follow focus solely on the actual occupations in the given context.

The group of craftsmen and related occupations is the only one of the Middle groups where the adjectives most often evaluate the occupations and not the discourse, or act as explanatory modifiers. The most influential co-occurrences in the positive classification are *slavný* 'famous' and *významný* 'important, significant' with *malíř* 'painter', which is one reason the ISCO 7 group's positivity is higher compared to the ISCO 6 and 8 around it. This is also enhanced by the normally rarer adjective *vynikající* 'excellent', which is the ninth most frequently used adjective in this group that modifies the noun, including the multifunctional *velký* 'great', *dobrý* 'good', and so on. In these most driving co-occurrences, we also find *kvalifikovaný* 'qualified' and *tradiční* 'traditional' with *řemeslník* 'craftsman, artisan', a noun whose eight out of ten modifiers are positively classified adjectives. Among the negative rankings for ISCO 7, we find several co-occurrences with the noun *silničář* 'road worker'. Apart from the multifunctional adjectives, the most frequent adjectives with road workers are *špatný* 'bad', *těžký* 'heavy, hard' and *silný* 'strong'. To a lesser extent, there is also the adjective *poškozený* 'damaged, impaired', which mainly concerns the roads they work on. Another noun recurring in the top five list of most common, negative co-occurrences is *kominík* 'chimney sweep', modified by the adjective *falešný* 'fake, false'. There have been several occasions where fraudulent chimney sweeps roamed the Czech countryside to earn money, which is reflected in the frequencies of this dataset and gives a negative representation of the occupation. One newspaper concluded in a subtitle that *Znát svého kominíka se vyplatí* 'It pays to know your chimney sweep',[22] meaning that otherwise, a fraudulent one may steal your money.

The Military group is decreasing in prominence after the 1990s, and in the three years 1991, 2008, and 2018, when the negativity and positivity were almost equal, the most common noun *voják* 'soldier' most frequently co-occurs with *zraněný*

---

[22] *Právo* 12 July 2007, sentence ID pr070712:138:2:1.

'injured' or *zabitý* 'killed, which are indeed often modifiers of the noun. However, the negatively classified adjective *válečný* 'war-' also adds to the general negativity for this group. It is noteworthy that the adjective *sebevražedný* 'suicidal' is co-occurring more with the noun *voják* 'soldier' (965 times) compared to any other occupational noun (top two, *policista* 'police officer', has 669 and top three, *ministr* 'minister' has 256 co-occurrences, of which only a handful or two are actual modifiers). The highest frequency of *sebevražedný* + *voják* as a proportion of all tokens in the corpus was in 2018, followed by 2014 and 2003. Upon closer examination of the corpus, it becomes apparent that this is often related to suicide bombings or attacks in which soldiers are involved, typically because the target is a military object. The negative discourse prosody (see Section 1) about soldiers is thus increased by these co-occurrences, even though they are not suicidal themselves. On the other hand, the highest positivity for this group is created by the adjective *základní* 'basic' or 'fundamental', which has been classified as positive in the Subjectivity Lexicon. It often co-occurs with *voják* because of the collocation *vojáci základní služby* 'soldiers in [basic] military service', which is a neutral representation rather than a positive one. Among the other positive adjectives co-occurring with the noun 'soldier', we also have *mírový* 'peace(ful)' and *bezpečnostní* 'secure, safe(ty)', mainly due to the presence of international UN peacekeeping forces and other peace missions. An example: *Naši vojáci působili v rámci mírových sil OSN v Mogadišu od 23. července.* 'Our soldiers have been operating in the framework of the UN peacekeeping force in Mogadishu since 23 July.' Both 'peace(ful)' and 'secure, safe(ty)' put the soldiers themselves in a more positive light on a wider dicourse level.

The most frequently occurring female nouns in this group are *manažerka* 'manager' and *vrchní sestra* 'charge nurse/head nurse' or 'nurse practitioner' for ISCO 1 and for ISCO 5 *modelka* 'female model' (classified as an 'Other Sales worker' in the ISCO descriptions). For the female manager, seven adjectives are equally frequent, seen throughout the whole time: *příjemný* 'nice, pleasant', *schopný* 'able', 'competent', *sociální* 'social', *špičkový* 'peak, high-', *tvrdý* 'hard', *úspěšný* 'successful' and *významný* 'important'. Except for the first, they are all adjectives that occur more often with men than women, as seen in Section 3. It is noteworthy that female managers are frequently represented as *schopný* 'able', 'competent' more than any other occupation where either a feminine noun is present in the dataset or women are known to be prominent, such as with teachers. For nurses, the most frequent adjectives are *sociální* 'social', *nemocný* 'sick' and *rehabilitační* 'rehabilitative', but also *záchranný* 'salvage/safety', *možný* 'feasible', *špatný* 'bad' and *příjemný* 'nice, pleasant'. The noun *modelka* 'female model' most frequently (and unsurprisingly) co-occurs with *krásný* 'beautiful', but also with other mainly positive adjectives such as *slavný* 'famous', *úspěšný* 'successful' and *půvabný* 'charming'. These co-occurrences are often (41 per cent) found in magazines, which means that a study only analysing daily newspapers would yield different results for the models. It is worth noting that *schopný* 'able', 'competent' and *možný* 'feasible' (but also sometimes 'plausible' and 'possible') are adjectives that are more frequent with men in general but rank highly (number five with nurses) when referring to women's occupations in these Middle groups. A comparison with the dataset used in Section 3 reveals that *manažerka* 'female manager' is indeed one of the absolutely most common female nouns modified by these adjectives.

Summarising these occupational groups, positive adjectives are mainly associated with artistic and handicraft-related occupations such as the nouns *malíř* 'painter' and *řemeslník* 'craftsman, artisan', and to a certain extent peacekeeping military operations, but also with competent female managers. The more negative adjectives are associated with more dangerous, heavier or dirtier occupations such as the nouns *voják* 'soldier', *policista* 'police officer' and *silničář* 'road worker'. At the same time, for the more frequently represented occupations in the dataset, the adjectives less often describe the occupations, and more often the discourse around them, such as *válečný* 'war-', or are explanatory modifiers, such as *záchranný* 'rescue-' in *ředitel záchranné služby* 'director of (the) rescue services'. In this case, the theory that service and supervisory functions would give a more frequent and positive media representation seems confirmed by the positive co-occurrences, while the negative adjectives more often concern the context more than the professions themselves.

2.5.3 The Lower Groups: ISCO 4, ISCO 6, ISCO 8 and ISCO 9

The following paragraphs concern the least prominent groups in the data. In these low-frequency groups, it can be noted that the adjectives more often modify the nouns directly rather than appearing as co-occurrences nearby. ISCO 4 stands out here, partly because clerks and similar support occupations are normally part of a higher social group than occupations from ISCO 6, 8 and 9, but also in a purely linguistical manner: the occupations of ISCO 4 are not also surnames.

The ISCO 4 group is dominated by the noun *úředník* 'clerk', which has more than twice as many co-occurrences as the second most frequent noun, *prodejce* 'salesperson, seller'. This group receives increased negative classification as time goes by, and in the two most negative years of the 2010s, the salespeople nouns are the most prominent among this group. This is mainly due to a debate on door-to-door salespeople, pedlars. At the time, this practice was still rather common, but there were calls for an amendment to the law. This resulted in media examples such as *Doplácíme na nekalou praxi nepoctivých prodejců dek či hrnců.* 'We are paying the price because of unfair practice conducted by dishonest sellers of blankets or pots.'[23] The clerk nouns also receive a large share of the negative classification due to the modifier *nízký*; in its comparative form, *nižší úředník* means junior clerk. But almost as common is the adjective *špatný* 'bad', followed in frequency order by *podezřelý* 'suspicious' and *obyčejný* 'ordinary', which all are frequently used throughout the period. On the other hand, the positivity accompanying clerk nouns, which is larger during the first years, seems to be focused on fewer adjectives. *Schopný* 'able, competent' is the most common, closely followed by *možný* 'feasible, possible' and the multifunctional *sociální* 'social'. These adjectives appear consistently throughout the period. Some of the seemingly positive *schopný* are, however, in a doubtful or even negative context. An example from the transition from communist times to capitalist times is an interview in *Mlada Fronta Dnes* with the Plzeň boss of the vehicle manufacturer Škoda who was quoted saying *Například z více než 1300 úředníků zbude jen 60 schopných, opravdu řídících pracovníků.* 'For example, out of more than 1,300 clerks, there will be only 60 capable workers left that are truly executives.'[24]

In the other less frequently mentioned groups, a methodological problem arises with surnames, such as Chmelař 'hop-grower', Horník 'miner' or Kočí 'coachman'. Upon closer examination of the corpus concordances, it becomes clear that, for example, at least half of the co-occurrences with the possible hop-growers actually refer to someone with that surname. For ISCO 8, the most commonly used modifier is connected to a surname: *boží* 'godly' or 'divine' is simply a geographical modifier of a politician, Jan Horník from the city Boží Dar, who has been active throughout the entire period covered by this Element. Out of the 71,000 mentions of this noun in the entire journalistic corpus, approximately 20,000 are about him or other Horníks and need to be ignored. Most of the group's most prominent nouns are, however, not names, and after some controls for which lemma is actually used, the results presented here are deemed valid.

Figure 6 shows a negative evaluation of the ISCO 6 group of Skilled Agricultural, Forestry and Fishery Workers initially, but recent years have seen a 70 per cent positive classification. The top five co-occurrences per year indicate a clear transformation of the country from a communist regime with collective farms. During the 1990s, the noun *zemědělec* 'farmer' frequently

---

[23] *Lidové noviny* 13 May 2013, sentence ID ln130513:1:10:2.
[24] *Mladá Fronta DNES* 4 November 1992, sentence ID mf921104:33:2:5.

appeared in the top five most frequent positive co-occurrences, but after 2003, it drops to lower frequencies. In the list of the top five most driving negative co-occurrences, *zemědělec* 'farmer' appears in four out of the top five positions during nine of the 29 years, as recently as 2012, and occupies at least two of the top five every year. Negative co-occurrences with *zemědělec* 'farmer' are less frequent than positive, and mostly relate to harvests. The adjective *nízký* 'low', followed by *špatný* 'bad', refers to events such as extreme weather that is harmful to farmers. Another common negative term is *postižený* 'affected', used in a similar context (e.g. ... *pomoc zemědělcům postiženým povodněmi* ... ' ... aid to farmers affected by floods ... ') which was very frequent in 2002. The negatively classified *poslední* 'last' appears frequently in a climate context to compare one year with previous years. As an experiment, I removed the ambiguous adjectives *nízký* 'low' and *poslední* 'last'. Consequently, the negative classification decreased significantly for the group (approximately 25 instead of 30 per cent over the last five years). I subsequently removed all three ambiguous adjectives (*nízký* 'low', *poslední* 'last' and *vášnivý* 'enthusiastic'), which did not change the ISCO group's evaluation significantly; the evaluation became only slightly less negative than in Figure 6.

In more recent years the most frequent and driving, positively classified, co-occurrences are instead dominated by the noun *rybář* 'fisher'. In the top five, the fisher nouns are modified with *úspěšný* 'successful' and *zkušený* 'experienced', but most of all with *vášnivý* 'passionate, enthusiastic'. This adjective is not commonly used to describe other occupational nouns. It is worth noting that these positively classified texts most often refer to people who fish in their spare time, rather than professional fishermen.

The ISCO 8 group has the title Plant and Machine Operators, and Assemblers, but also includes some other types of 'operators', generally considered drivers. The most frequent noun overall is *horník* 'miner' (which is a surname in several cases, as described earlier), followed by *taxikář* 'taxi driver'. Among the positive adjectives, a religious adjective appears among the most frequent co-occurrences, namely *svatý* 'holy'. Due to the high risk involved in mining, there are many saints for both miners and mining, and their images or statues are often present in mining workplaces.[25] While these saints are reflected in the news and contribute to the context, they do not directly modify the miner nouns. Balancing this positivity are adjectives about the dangerous work in mines. In 1992, *horník*

---

[25] One example: *Nad pracemi v podzemí bude bdít patronka horníků svatá Barbora. Její dřevěnou sošku stavbaři uložili do ocelové nerezové klece a spustili do těžní šachty.* 'Barbora, the patron saint of miners, will watch over the work below ground. Her wooden statue was placed in a steel stainless steel cage and lowered into the mine shaft.' *Lidové noviny* 12 September 2007, sentence ID ln070912:68:5:1.

'mineworker' is most often modified by *postižený* 'impaired' and *poškozený* 'damaged, injured' that create the extra negativity. Both adjectives were used in articles about adjusting the remuneration for disabled miners, a highly debated topic that year. Miners are once more in focus in 1999, but this time with the adjectival modifier *zraněný* 'hurt, injured'. The news value increased that year due to an earthquake that had a severe impact on a mine near Ostrava. In addition, the dataset includes the adjective *uvězněný* 'imprisoned' or 'trapped', adding to the discourse of mining as a dangerous occupation. The noun *horník* 'mineworker' is the most commonly co-occurring noun with this adjective.

Two general nouns dominate the final ISCO 9 group: *dělník* 'worker', which mainly receives negative evaluations, and *pomocník* 'helper, assistant', that mainly receives positive evaluations. Of the 113,015 co-occurrences in the dataset, 51,528 include the former and 30,124 the latter. *Kočí* 'coachman' which is most often a surname, is a distant third, followed by *uklízečka* 'female cleaner' – one of very few female occupations in the most frequent co-occurrences. The negative co-occurrences are dominated by *dělník* 'worker', and in second place is *pomocník* 'helper, assistant'. In this ISCO group of unqualified occupations, the noun *dělník* 'worker' is frequently modified by *nekvalifikovaný* 'unqualified'.[26] Other common modifiers include *obyčejný* 'ordinary' and *ochotný* 'willing, co-operative'.

The positive co-occurrences are reversely dominated by *pomocník* 'helper, assistant' before *dělník* 'worker', and no other nouns enter the top five. When expanded to the top ten most frequent co-occurrences, the female worker *dělnice* squeezes in twice during the 1990s (the adjectives being *krásný* 'beautiful' and *vhodný* 'suitable';[27] see Section 3.3). The reason we do not see the female cleaner here, despite *uklízečka* being a comparatively prominent noun, is that the distance is wider between the co-occurrences of noun and adjective – the adjusted sentiment value is not high enough for the female cleaners.

Summarising, the adjectives often describe the workers or their occupational hazards. They did not reflect any occupational pride nor positive community feeling; instead, the positivity often came from enthusiastic hobby representations or the presence of saints. As regards the theory on giving service to others

---

[26] It should be noted that during the whole timespan, the non-negated lemma, *kvalifikovaný* 'qualified', is used only one time less than the negated.

[27] *Dnes se přece nosí skoro všechno, móda je velmi tolerantní. Určitá pravidla však přesto existují. Něco jiného je vhodné pro dělnice, něco jiného pro pracovnice v zemědělství či prodavačky, někde se nosí pracovní stejnokroje.* 'Today, almost everything may be worn, there is a large tolerance for what is labelled fashion. However, there are some rules. Some garments are suitable for female workers, others for farm workers or shop assistants, and in some places, they must wear work uniforms.' *Lidové noviny – Nedělní příloha* (Sunday edition) no. 47 1991, sentence ID: lnnp9147:20:3:4.

leading to more frequent and more positive media representation, it cannot be confirmed here. Perhaps the lack of a supervisory function is the key to this, something that a future study could assess in greater detail. Finally, over time it became clear how the significance of farmers has changed after 1989, and the influence of climate change on the country become apparent through reports on their crops.

2.6 Summary of the Stratification of Occupations

The significance of supervision and, to a certain extent, providing service in obtaining positive news representation appears to outweigh other factors. Two groups that have supervisory functions and provide service to the general public, Managers (1) and Craft and Related Trades (7), receive the most positive representation. However, the positivity towards the latter group often stems from nouns for craftspeople and famous, dead painters. The Elementary Occupations (9) are among the least mentioned, although that particular group only has a moderate number of co-occurrences that are classified as negative. Another finding is that the overrepresented Military group (0) seems to receive a more positive evaluation over time, using the adjective classification of the Subjectivity Lexicon. During peacetime, the military often have both a supervisory function and provide service to the general public. Finally, the group with the most negative representation is the non-ISCO group that includes politicians and a few other independent titles. All nouns in this group are considered newsworthy and are therefore often mentioned, but it is difficult to pinpoint the evaluation from a bird's-eye perspective. The evaluation overall is, however, consistent with the loss in prestige found by Tuček (2019). To summarise, the hypothesis that occupations with lower levels of education and income (ISCO groups 7–9) would be less frequent and more negatively evaluated in the material is only partially verified, but the famous people in ISCO 7 strengthen the hypothesis of people of higher socio-economic status having a greater news presence. Finally, the Elementary Occupations (9) include many occupations that provide services to the general public, and the positivity of the group's main service giver, *pomocník* 'helper, assistant', seems to verify this Element's theory on the importance of service provision for creating a positive representation. Their lack of supervisory functions may then be a reason for their low frequency.

Some differences are identified when comparing the evaluative frequency with the Prestige list (Tuček 2019). This list includes occupations from all ISCO groups except 8, which is the only group that ever reaches over 50 per cent negative classification. Additionally, the list is dominated by the Professionals

(2), which includes journalists. The prestige of this profession decreases over time, but this is not reflected in consistently more negative co-occurrences after 2011. Managers (1) fall in both the prestige ranking and the number of evaluated occurrences; as their prestige declines, their number of mentions in the news does so too, even if the positivity stays high. Thus, it would appear that perceived prestige does not necessarily correlate with positive evaluations in the news press.

From a longitudinal stratification and equality perspective, it seems the two ISCO groups closest to the journalists and editors that produced the source texts, Professionals (2) and Technicians and Associate Professionals (3), are the norm throughout the period, which is also supported by the Professionals dominating the titles in the Prestige list. In terms of evaluation, there is very little difference between these two groups over time, and their frequency in these news media also correlates best with the number of employees. Their evaluation needed closer scrutiny, due to the large number of professions in the group, which revealed that some of the positivity was in the context rather than modifying the actual occupational nouns. In the most negatively evaluated group, the politicians and business owners, the balance between positivity and negativity was rather consistent. The primary difference over time found in that group was that business owners were mentioned more often in a financial or economical context in the 1990s but in later years more often in an event-based context. In contrast to previous research for Norway, the results for Czech media show that nurses of different types (groups 1 and 2) are not evaluated less frequently over time. Also contrary to research from other countries, the frequency of Elementary Occupations (9) in Czech news media has not decreased significantly in recent years. Finally, the co-occurring results only showed a few occupations with a female form (competent managers, nice teachers, kind nurses and beautiful workers). Since this is partly due to grammatical androcentrism (if there is one man in the group, then the grammatical form is masculine), Section 3 on gender has a differently constructed dataset, where cleaners are also included.

3 The Representation of Gendered Nouns

The significance of gender equality for society is highlighted in policy documents produced both globally and regionally. For instance, the United Nations Sustainable Development Goals emphasise that 'Gender equality is not only a fundamental human right, but a necessary foundation for a peaceful, prosperous and sustainable world' (United Nations n/a) and the European Union guidelines advise that all actors are to strive to obtain a balance in 'gender, geography and career stage' (European Commission 2019: 8–9). The news press of Czechia is investigated in this section to determine whether the guidelines set by the United Nations and the European Union are being followed. According to Baker's (2014) diachronic overview (92–93), gender research using various English-based corpora suggests that there has been a shift in how women and men are referred to in the media, but that the prevailing norm remains to use masculine nouns. The phenomenon of othering can here be observed when one gender is represented by clearly distinct adjectives compared to the other gender in this section, particularly when it comes to adjectives describing their roles in society.

This section covers a wider period than most other studies on gender in language – exceptions include Baker (2014) and Stefanowitsch and Middeke (2023). Additionally, it introduces another tool to the methodology: the semantic categories created by researchers from the Lancaster University Centre for Computer Corpus Research on Language (UCREL).[28] These categories consist of English words that were later translated into Czech and other languages as described in Piao et al. (2016). The decision to use these categories was based on the one hand on Lei and Liu's (2021: 1) statement that many researchers combine 'subjectivity, polarity, and semantic orientation' to find sentiment, and on the other hand on the observation that the Czech language often describes women using appearance-related adjectives.

Androcentrism is a recurring term in this section, and means the fact that men or a masculine grammatical form are the norm. Czech is a language comprising three genders (feminine, masculine and neuter) for nominal parts of speech and some verbal forms, and an extra, 'animate' for masculine creatures.[29] According to Čmejrková (2003), in her general overview in English of the grammatical genders of Czech, readers of Czech are accustomed to the masculine normative form, whether in singular or plural (48), unless reading a text specifically targeted at women or girls. Currently, there is no consensus on equal linguistic treatment in Czech (53), such as the English use of the singular *they* or the Spanish use of a slash between the gender markers, such as *amigo/a*.

Several studies have been conducted on gender representation in different countries, including close-reading analyses (e.g. Barát 2005; Hedin 2007; Ibroscheva & Raicheva-Stover 2009). These studies suggest that women are

---

[28] https://ucrel.lancs.ac.uk. [Accessed 22 March 2024].

[29] This study is not about self-identified or non-binary gender, since it is primarily focused on grammatically gendered nouns. Czech is a highly flexible language with, for example, seven nominal cases, but non-binary gendered persons still do not have a grammatical form that is used throughout the language (see e.g. Kolek & Valdrová 2020 or Thál & Elmerot 2022 for more on grammatical gender studies of Czech).

often portrayed negatively, with positive modifiers mainly referring to appearance or sexuality. Barát also notes negative coverage in the Hungarian data, based on the idea that women's equality was something argued for by the communists and therefore viewed negatively in the post-communist country. Coffey-Glover (2019), on the other hand, examined the portrayal of British men in women's magazines. The study found that men were primarily identified by their occupational roles, and adjectival descriptions of men more commonly referred to personality traits or behavioural qualities rather than physical appearance (215–216). Thus, her study confirms that men in different Indo-European languages are evaluated less frequently by their appearance than women.

In Czechia, Kadlecová (2010) analysed five articles from 'exclusive' Czech women's magazines and examined the ideological perspectives presented. She concluded that in 2000, there was very negative coverage of women (62–63, 100), particularly when women from the Social Democrats formed a 'shadow government of women' due to the absence of women in the country's parliamentary government (see Section 2.5.1 for more on the adjective 'shadow'). Havelková (2017: 305–306) notes that the European Union (EU)[30] has been the primary catalyst for positive legal changes for women, probably due to the principle of gender mainstreaming (see Weiner & MacRae 2017: 74). Conversely, the Czech government has implemented negative changes, including reduced social welfare for collective childcare, common taxation of spouses, and legal punishments for prostitutes but not their clients (186). In this context, Fojtová (2016: 115) claims that around 2005 the same mainstream press that had previously ridiculed feminism 'began to publish pro-feminist articles'.[31] Borovanská (2012) acknowledges that the term 'feminism' is no longer taboo in Czech public discourse. However, she notes that female politicians interviewed in the news tend to accept the disadvantages they face, such as being responsible for childcare and receiving comments on their appearance, as a matter of fact rather than something to fight against. These observations suggest that there is still a long way to go in achieving gender equality in politics.

Corpus-assisted or otherwise quantitative studies often reach the same conclusion. Šonková (2011) agrees with Hedin (2007) that there are more emotions in the expressions used by and about women than those used by and about men in their Czech data. Caldas-Coulthard and Moon (2010) studied adjectives modifying nouns such as 'woman' and 'man' in British newspapers and noted substantial asymmetry, including that women are described in terms of physical

---

[30] Czechia became a member of the European Union on 1 May 2004.
[31] Unfortunately, she does not provide any examples in that chapter.

appearance more often than men are. Baker (2014: 150) also observes andro-centrism, but states that girls are represented more positively than boys in his longitudinal corpora.[32] Pantić (2017) analysed a Serbian corpus[33] for noun and adjective co-occurrences and found that female nouns received a larger share of subjective evaluations. Rao and Taboada (2021) conducted a detailed study using unsupervised topic modelling, although sentiment was not taken into account. Their Canadian study found that feminine nouns were more frequently used in caregiving contexts, while masculine nouns were more common in political and business contexts. Their methodological model could be refined, as suggested by the critique of this method in Brookes and McEnery (2019: 18), and reused for future studies. Garcia-Blanco and Wahl-Jorgensen (2012) con-cluded, based on data from four European countries, that press coverage patterns reinforce the construction of female politicians as deviating from the norm by focusing on their appearance and traditional gender roles, following the 2012 election of a female-majority cabinet in Spain. This could also be seen as a comment on Section 2 on occupations in this Element.

Additionally, similar data has been used in other studies. Elmerot (2017) used a previous version of the same corpus used in this Element with sentiment values translated from the Harvard Psychosociological Dictionary (Kelly & Stone 1975, 10; 12–13). The results indicated that women were only portrayed more positively than men in occupations where they are the norm, such as teachers. Zasina's (2019) analysis of the nouns *muž* 'man' and *žena* 'woman' is another study relevant to this section. He uses another journalistic corpus dating from 2010 to 2014 and notes a wider range of adjectives (100) modifying men than women (46), despite starting with a similar number of nouns for both genders. Daily newspapers (tabloids, broadsheets and regional newspapers) represent men more negatively than women, while magazines have positive sentiments towards both genders. In his data, men were defined by age, strength, appearance and committed crimes, whereas women were defined by mother-hood, attractiveness and victimisation, but also often by their nationality (310).

In summary, previous studies from several regions show unequal representa-tion of women in relation to men through highlighting different attributes for men and women. Women are more frequently defined by evaluative modifying adjec-tives in both spoken and written data, where seemingly positive words may in fact be cases of linguistic othering. The typical example is 'beautiful', suggesting that women who are not beautiful are abnormal. In addition, family classifications

---

[32] He used the Corpus of Historic American English, 400 million words from the years 1810 to 2009.

[33] Corpus of Contemporary Serbian Language (SrpKor2013), 122 million words from the years 1991 to 2012.

may suggest that men are incapable of caring for children. This section will examine how this asymmetrical representation is also valid for this dataset.

3.1 Research Questions and Aim

Previous research paves the way for the hypothesis:

If androcentrism is the norm, then nouns referring to women may be expected to co-occur with evaluative adjectives more frequently than nouns referring to men. Additionally, if equal representation of women and men has increased in recent years due to social change, the number of positively and negatively evaluated co-occurrences for both genders in the dataset would be more balanced towards 2018.

The aim of this analysis is to determine whether women and men are equally represented, or if the linguistic othering is prominent. This section therefore poses three main research questions:

1. Are women more frequently described with adjectives related to appearance, as suggested by previous research?
2. To what extent do evaluative adjectives differ in the representation of the genders?
3. How have these representations evolved in the post-1989 period?

Once these questions have been answered, it will be possible to confirm or reject arguments from previous research using the data and methods presented. It will also uncover new insights into the representation of women and men in Czech news media.

3.2 Data Extraction from the Corpus

The dataset used for this section comprises 7.87 million of the observations described in the introduction – all feminine nouns and the closest masculine equivalents of the feminine nouns (see Section 3.3.1) with their co-occurring adjectives. The analyses in this section, as well as throughout the entire Element, are based on the lemmatised forms of the words, which allows for the inclusion of all possible word forms. Of the 773 adjectives in the Subjectivity Lexicon, 724 were found in the corpus co-occurring with the masculine nouns and 720 with the feminine nouns in this section.[34]

The main issue in this section concerns the selection of female form nouns. In his 2014 book, Baker (2014, 74) notes that analyses of gender representation need a large corpus to produce a cumulative picture of views in the society and

---

[34] The adjectives that were only co-occuring with men were *rektifikovaný* 'rectified', *obohacovací* 'enriching', *katalytický* 'catalytic' and *dehumanizující* 'dehumanising'.

time in question. In the same book, he published an impressively long timeline (1800–2010) of the words *man* and *woman* from an American English corpus, where *man* was more frequently used throughout, although it decreased as *woman* increased towards the end of the 1900s (Baker 2014: 79). Baker suggests that a variety of words for both men and women should be used to provide a more comprehensive analysis. Therefore, the largest available Czech thesaurus (Klégr 2007) was used when compiling the words for this study. The entry noun *člověk* 'human being' (grammatically masculine) was used as selection criterion, and even though the noun *osoba*, 'person' (grammatically feminine) is included in that entry, the resulting list of nouns was found to include a larger number referring to men than to women. This androcentrism, or male bias, is in line with the previous research mentioned earlier. The same finding was made when adding the ISCO occupational titles (see Section 2.3). The main reason for the latter is that the masculine form is considered the norm in Czech, to the extent that there is no alternative 'linguistic treatment' provided in these noun lists. If all the 'human being' nouns in the thesaurus were used as corpus search terms, there would be an inbuilt bias towards the masculine.

The design decision in this section is to select the feminine nouns listed in the thesaurus and their closest masculine equivalents, rather than all masculine nouns. This ensures consistency and avoids arbitrary selection. This means that if *bába* 'grandma' is in the list, so is *děda* 'grandpa', or if *učitelka* 'female teacher' is there, so is *učitel* 'male teacher'. In practice, all the nationality names appear in the list because they have both masculine and feminine forms, whereas few occupational titles appear, compared to the whole dataset used in this Element, because they have no feminine form in the original sources. Additionally, some feminine nouns had to be omitted because there are no masculine equivalents in the language. These include for example *madona* 'madonna', *porodní asistentka* 'midwife' and *staniční sestra* (approximately) 'charge nurse' or 'head nurse'.[35] This was the preferred option, given the male bias of the dataset. Eventually, similarly to Zasina (2019: 303), using an equal number of masculine and feminine nouns resulted in a higher number of masculine adjective–noun co-occurrences. This may be attributed to the use of lemmata, which includes some plural forms that are gender neutral. Unfortunately, no other option was available for the news corpora at the time, as they were not syntactically annotated. The option to use co-occurrences in singular only was rejected, based on the fact that it would give a biased reflection of the language in news media.

---

[35] Both the equivalent occupational titles *porodní asistent* and *staniční bratr* exist, albeit with few examples, in the corpus, but not in the ISCO lists.

Since this section aims in part to extend the work of Zasina (2019), who focuses on the lemmata *žena* 'woman' and *muž* 'man', the absolute frequency of these two nouns was calculated for the current dataset. There are 723,611 *žena* (42.6 per cent of the feminine nouns) and 766,750 *muž* (12.4 per cent of the masculine nouns) over time co-occurring with these evaluative adjectives. Out of all co-occurrences of adjectives with *žena*, the top three are every year with the overall most frequent adjectives (*velký* 'large, big', *dobrý* 'good' and *poslední* 'last'). In the top 25 of the most frequent female noun+adjective co-occurrences in this dataset, only three nouns manage to break the dominance of *žena*: *sociální+pracovnice* (most often a bigram, 'female social worker'), *základní+učitelka* (most often *učitelka základní školy* 'female teacher of the early school years') and *velký+starostka* 'large/big' + 'female mayor'. In the last case, the adjective is such a multifunctional word, that it rarely has to do with the mayor herself, but occurs in the vicinity, such as *Šternberská starostka / NN/ se* <u>*velkou*</u> *měrou zasloužila o to, že město převzalo záruku za úvěr 600 000 korun* 'The female Mayor of Šternberg /NN/ was to a <u>large</u> extent responsible for the fact that the city took over the guarantee for a loan of CZK 600,000.'[36] Such co-occurrences are weighted lower in the analyses (see Section 1.3.5). This may point to a general othering of women in that they are not mentioned in as many roles. In the top 25 of the most frequent male noun+adjective co-occurrences in this dataset, there are more nouns: *ministr* 'minister', *policista* 'police officer', *manažer* 'manager' and *lékař* 'physician', in addition to the equivalents of the female nouns just mentioned. The two nationalities *Čech* 'Czech' and *Němec* 'German' are also apparent in the more diverse top list of masculine nouns. The adjectives do not differ greatly, but *podezřelý* 'suspicious, suspected' is more influential for the masculine nouns. The representation of men about taking part in criminal activities could point to an othering, but this adjective often occurs with police-related nouns.

In Czech, adjectives are usually negated by prefixing, resulting in adjectival pairs such as *šťastný* 'happy' and *nešťastný* 'unhappy'. When the Subjectivity Lexicon of Czech was created, this feature was described as being problematic (Veselovská 2017: 77). This re-surfaced for this study since the lemmata include both affirmative and negated word forms. To address this, a specific variable was added to the database indicating the presence of negation in the original text.

In some of the analyses, four of the most frequent multifunctional adjectives (Cvrček et al. 2020: 122) were removed from the data to determine which adjectives actually made a difference. It is noted in the analyses if they were

---

[36] *Mladá fronta DNES* 19 August 1992, corpus sentence ID mf920819:95:2:1.

removed. The four adjectives are *velký* 'large, big', *dobrý* 'good', *poslední* 'last' and *rád* 'glad/like'. The last one is mainly used in the expression *Mám ráda . . .* 'I like . . . ' as in *Ze zimních sportů mám ráda lyžování . . .* 'Of the winter sports, I like skiing . . . '.

Finally, it must be noted that the word *sestra*, 'sister' (a total of 4.85 per cent for the feminine nouns) is categorised as an occupational title rather than a family member, due to its multiple meanings. It is the second most frequent noun for women, and thus the driving force behind the high proportion of occupational titles. The collocation tool available at the Czech National Corpus interface confirms that this appears to be a reasonable choice. Apart from modal verbs, prepositions, and conjugations, frequent collocations for this word (with a collocation window span of one to the left and right)[37] in the used sub-corpus are lemmata such as *nemocnice* 'hospital', *lékař* 'physician' and *oddělení* 'ward'.

3.3 Analyses of the Gender Data

Aggregated data, as used here, need various analyses to return more robust answers to the research questions posed. In this section, there are three groups of analyses. The first is an analysis of the nouns, categorised into five different groups of human nouns. The second group of analyses is based on the adjectives, and their classification according to the Subjectivity Lexicon for Czech, as described in Section 1.3. For the third group of analyses, the adjectives co-occurring with the feminine nouns have been divided into semantic categories,[38] methodologically inspired by Islentyeva's (2018) study on the difference between collostructions of the words 'migrant' and 'immigrant', and Zasina's (2019) study on adjectives with 'woman' and 'man'.

3.3.1 Noun Categories

The noun analysis reveals the proportions of nouns in each of five proposed categories (see what follows). This was carried out to enable comparison with previous research by Coffey-Glover (2019) and to a certain extent also Havelková (2017), Barát (2005) and Ibroscheva and Raicheva-Stover (2009).

---

[37] With 1 to each side: www.korpus.cz/kontext/collx?viewmode=kwic&pagesize=1000&attrs=word& attr_vmode=visible-kwic&base_viewattr=word&refs=%3Ddoc.title&q=~nOIIYQAqwUiE&cattr= lemma&cfromw=1&ctow=1&cminfreq=10&cminbgr=1&cbgrfns=m&cbgrfns=t&cbgrfns=d&c sortfn=f&collpage=1.

[38] As Stubbs noted (2002: 89), 'semantics deals with how linguistic signs relate to the external world'. Two examples of semantic groups are 'vehicles' that would include the nouns 'tram' and 'bicycle', or 'animal likeness', where 'hawkeye' would be placed when it means a person with keen sight.

It also considers the historical context of women being the core of the family (e.g. Feinberg 2006a,b), as described in Section 1.2.1. Mahlberg (2005: 102) structured the people nouns in her study into similar categories, albeit based on meaning in her (English) corpus. In this section, the category 'family' is similar to her meaning 1, and includes generic nouns for men (*muži*), women (*ženy*) and family members. The five categories, partially informed by pre-existing variables for nationality and occupation, are ranked according to frequency, and frequency of modification by evaluative adjectives, in the dataset.

Consequently, one variable in the dataset comprises the subsequent five categories (listed here with four examples each): family members, FAM, e.g. *žena* 'woman/wife', *babička* 'granny', *muž* 'man/husband', *dědeček* 'granddad'; humans in general, HUM, for example *dáma* 'lady', *důchodkyně* 'female pensioner', *světák* 'man of the world', *důchodce* 'male pensioner'; nationalities, NAT, for example *Norka* 'female Norwegian', *Syřanka* 'female Syrian', *Nor* 'male Norwegian', *Syřan* 'male Syrian'; occupational titles, PRO, for example *soudkyně* 'female judge', *prodavačka* 'saleswoman', *soudce* 'male judge', *prodavač* 'salesman'; and religious affiliations, REL, for example *Židovka* 'female Jew', *ateistka* 'female atheist', *Žid* 'male Jew', *ateista* 'male atheist'.

Table 7 shows the number of female and male nouns co-occurring with evaluative adjectives, aggregated over the whole period. The percentages in table 7 show that women are referred to as family members (FAM) in about the same proportion as men are referred to as professionals (PRO); in each case accounting for about 50 per cent of the female and male nouns, respectively. The second most common noun category for women in Czech media is their occupational role (just over 30 per cent). The men in this dataset have a more even distribution than women of other categories than their occupation (approximately 15, 11 and 21 per cent for FAM, HUM and NAT, respectively).

The most common nouns *žena* (43 per cent of the feminine nouns over the whole period) and *muž* (12 per cent of all the masculine nouns) are included in the category FAM, for family, following Mahlberg (2005: 100). They mean both 'woman' and 'wife', both 'man' and 'husband', respectively. Both *žena* and *muž* account for just over 80 per cent of the FAM category co-occurrences for their respective genders. This is expected as these nouns have multifunctional uses and can also refer to biological differences in Czech. Even if half of the occurrences of these two nouns[39] were in FAM and the other half in HUM, the ranking in Table 7 would remain unchanged. The exact proportions need to be investigated further. The term for 'human', *člověk* has been excluded from

---

[39]   In total, there were 561,782 co-occurrences of *žena* and 82,651 co-occurrences with *muž*.

Table 7 Noun categories used and their number of sampling points in the Gender dataset.

Noun category	Nr of female co-occurrences	Percentage female	Nr of male co-occurrences	Percentage male
FAM (family members)	863,096	50.83 %	935,939	15.15 %
PRO (occupational titles)	535,566	31.54 %	3,169,449	51.32 %
HUM (humans in general)	161,829	9.53 %	684,099	11.08 %
NAT (nationalities or ethnicities)	134,445	7.92 %	1,300,536	21.06 %
REL (religious persons)	3,208	0.19 %	86,266	1.40 %
Total	1,698,144	100.00 %	6,176,289	100.00 %

the sample in this section. It refers to any kind of human, despite its masculine grammatical gender (Čmejrková 2003: 33), and has the category HUM in the larger dataset.

Table 3 suggests that the men are predominantly referred to by their occupation (51.32 per cent) while the women are referred to as family members (50.83 per cent). The masculine nouns are also referred to using a wider perspective: the second highest category, NAT for nationalities, accounts for slightly over one-fifth, 21 per cent, of the total, two for 11–16 per cent and only one (religious affiliation) for less than 10 per cent. The nouns in the PRO category are analysed more closely in Section 2.4 and the NAT categories in Section 1.4. In contrast to men, the women maintain professional status (PRO) as their secondary most frequent category, making up nearly a third of the total feminine nouns. Within the dataset, the most frequently occurring PRO nouns among women include *učitelka* 'teacher', *starostka* 'mayor', *pracovnice* 'female worker', *ministryně* 'minister' and *modelka* 'female model'. They are all in the top ten most frequent for women. For men, the top ten includes more occupations, of which the top five are *starosta* 'mayor', *ministr* 'minister', *policista* 'police officer', *lékař* 'physician' and *pracovník* 'male worker'. Teachers are undoubtedly more often women than men in Czechia (up until

1999, see Weiner 2007: 34), and women are claimed to get a more positive representation in the Czech news when they dominate an occupation (Elmerot 2017). While teachers still claim high prestige in Czech society (numbers 3 and 4 on the 'Prestige list' since 2011, see Tuček 2019 and Section 2.2), the occupations of policemen and physicians are more clearly linked to prestige and power than the occupations of teachers and models.

Figures 10 and 11 display the distribution of these noun categories over time in the dataset, co-occurring with evaluative adjectives. The ratio of the frequency of the categories remains fairly constant over time.

These two figures have a *y*-axis showing the number of occurrences relative to the total number of tokens in the sub-corpus used for this Element, to see changes in frequency over time. Having the relative number of tokens per year on the *y*-axis makes it a comparison with the whole population, to see whether the frequency of the noun categories increases or decreases compared to the whole population of news texts (see the corpus constitution in Section 1.3.4). In these cases, there are no overlaps between the evaluated noun categories.[40] For the men, the occupational category (PRO) is the most prominent throughout the entire period (see Figure 11), and for the women, the most prominent is the family category (FAM), followed by the occupational category (PRO), (see Figure 11). We may, however, note the different scales for the genders, which shows that even the most frequent category for women in Figure 10, the family category (FAM), with frequencies at best between 150 and 210 per million tokens, would only be ranked third or fourth in relative frequency if placed alongside the masculine sample points of Figure 11. Nevertheless, the overall slightly upward trend for the female and the downward trend for the male co-occurrences are partly due to the evaluation as such and will be discussed further in Section 3.3.3.

Thus, in Figure 10, women are most often evaluated as a family member (FAM) over time; the trend line rises steadily after the initial year with few sources until its peak in the year 2000. In part, this might be explained by the contents of the corpus, where more media types are added that may have a larger interest in writing about women as well as men, such as certain lifestyle magazines. Additionally, the content of the constant news sources in the corpus changes; see Section 3.3.3. Occupational titles (PRO) form the second most frequent category. On the other hand, in Figure 11 men have a much wider gap between the category PRO and their second most frequent category, nationalities (NAT). The three categories NAT, HUM and FAM are closer to each other,

---

[40] The graphs of the categories show the number of adjective + noun co-occurrences in this dataset over time, not nouns alone.

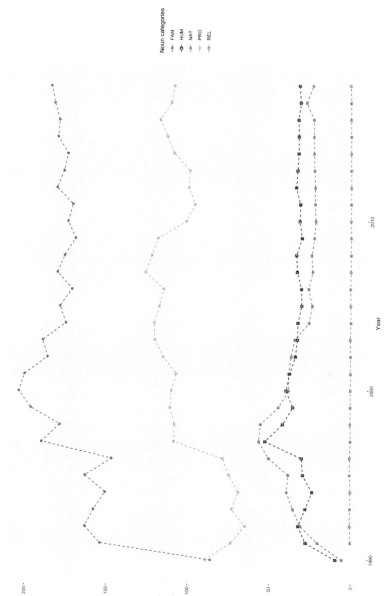

Figure 10 Noun categories per year for female nouns, relative to tokens in the sub-corpus.

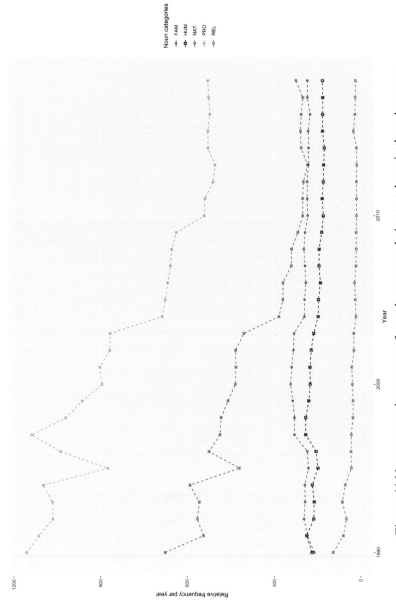

Figure 11 Noun categories per year for male nouns, relative to tokens in the sub-corpus.

and further from the PRO category than in the graph for feminine noun categories. This indicates that men are mentioned more frequently with their job title than anything else. The trend lines of these broad categories generally confirm previous studies (e.g. Zasina 2019; Elmerot 2017). In Czech news, women are described from a relational perspective more often than men, but their occupational role is also important as a part of the whole picture.

3.3.2 Analyses Based on the Subjectivity Lexicon

This section provides an overview of the entire period using aggregated and partially separated data. Previous research rarely indicates whether women or men receive positive evaluations in the media, whether in Czech or other languages. Studies that do draw such conclusions mainly focus on a limited number of nouns for women and men, whereas this study offers a broader perspective.

The method used here stems from the premise that each year is a representative sample of the population of mainstream printed media of Czechia. As the number of sources grow, so does the corpus. The proportion of masculine and feminine co-occurrences within these years reflects linguistic changes in society and politics in that specific year. The summed sentiment is relativised in the graphs first by dividing it with the summed number of evaluated frequencies per issue and year (see Figure 12). Balancing out the amounts of gendered co-occurrences in this way helps to determine which gender is more positively evaluated. The sentiment values are then further normalised by the number of tokens per year in the corpus (see Figures 13–15).

Evaluation in the Whole Dataset

The increasing or decreasing frequency of evaluation is shown in Figure 12, using all the Subjectivity lexicon's evaluative adjectives. This relates to the research questions by showing which groups – women or men – are more evaluated in the dataset, by positive and negative adjectives, respectively, and which trends are visible when looking at the evaluative aspect of language as a whole – thus combining the two facets. Figure 12 should be read as a balanced dataset, consisting of equal amounts of female and male co-occurrences, in an attempt to visually remove the androcentrism. It was created by dividing the summed adjusted sentiment value (see Section 1.3.5) with the total number of actual co-occurrences in this dataset. The evaluation is then presented in Figure 12 by positive (bright green) and negative (dark red) classification, respectively.

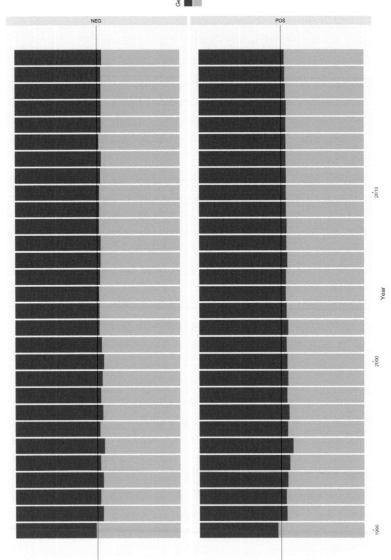

Figure 12 Proportion of positive (bright green) and negative (dark red) sentiment per year and gender in the dataset.

Figure 12 indicates that the women in my data are evaluated more in magazines and newspapers combined. Both the positive and negative facets reveal a larger proportion of female evaluation. However, we see that the positivity (bottom facet) decreases with time, whereas the negativity (top facet) only decreases slightly after 2001, then stays rather stable, and does not increase until after 2013. Therefore, the hypothesis that the women in this dataset are evaluated more than the men appears verified.

In contrast, the co-occurrences in Figure 13 are calculated relative to the total number of tokens in the corpus of newspapers and magazines (NMG) from which they were extracted. They reveal the amount of male versus female evaluated co-occurrences each year. Had there been an equal amount of feminine and masculine evaluated co-occurrences, the bars would have been equally long.

Figure 13 reveals that masculine co-occurrence forms dominate throughout every year, indicating a high level of androcentrism. Additionally, it shows that women are both evaluated and mentioned more over time, occupying a larger proportion of the co-occurrences in later years. Combined, the two facets together demonstrate that the average Czech who has been reading newspapers and magazines since 1990 should become increasingly accustomed to women being (evaluatively) represented in the news.

Notably, there is a significant increase in positivity in 1995. Upon analysing the differences in adjectives between 1994, 1995 and 1996,[41] it appears they are not based on a specific event or a specific person, but on the corpus behind the dataset, where the lifestyle weekly magazine *Vlasta* was introduced in 1995 and then removed again. It would be expected that women were represented in a more positive light in a magazine like *Vlasta*.[42] The co-occurrences with the most positive impact from this magazine in 1995 include *hodný* + *babička* 'nice + grandmother', *úspěšný* + *žena* 'successful + woman' and *skvělý* + *švadlena* 'excellent female dressmaker'. These co-occurrences appear frequently.

In summary, these quantitative analyses show that female nouns are slightly more likely to be accompanied by evaluative adjectives than male nouns. This lends support to the proposition that women are evaluated more than men. In addition, the proportion of positive evaluations for female nouns has been observed to decline over time, while the prevalence of negative evaluations has remained relatively constant until 2013, when it began to increase. Furthermore, the analyses demonstrate that masculine nouns are the most prevalent and that they exert a dominant influence on an annual basis, indicating

---

[41] Files with the adjectives and their differences available at https://osf.io/xzpju/?view_only=c-b0ee3c198134174b0440f59095743c7 .

[42] *Vlasta* was founded in 1947 by feminist and anti-totalitarian lawyer Milada Horáková.

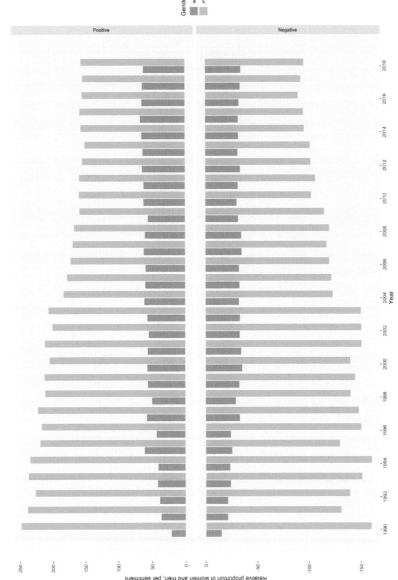

Figure 13 Relative frequency and sentiment classifications for the female (red) and male (blue) gendered co-occurrences per year.

a high degree of androcentrism. When considered together, the two analyses indicate that there has indeed been inequality in the evaluation of women and men in the Czech printed news media during these three decades.

3.3.3 Analyses Based on the Semantic Categorisations

Semantic categories are groups of words with a common denominator, which in turn gives the category its name. Some category examples are *Evaluation: good/bad* including words like *atrocious* or *creditable*, and *Judgement of appearance* including words like *pretty* or *bleak*. Since so few of the adjectives in the Subjectivity Lexicon were included in the classification made by Zasina (2019), the semantic categorisation for Czech created at UCREL (see Piao et al., 2016) was used instead. More adjectives from this study were included there than in Zasina's study, but 94 out of the 720 adjectives used with feminine nouns (and 98 of the 724 for men) had to be categorised manually for this study,[43] following the UCREL Semantic Analysis System guide (Archer et al. 2002) as closely as possible.[44] The semantics of the adjectives is merely touched upon here, since the analytical perspective is intended to pave the way for future studies. It must be noted that some categorisations may not be immediately clear and require further discussion in more detailed studies.

Table 8 shows examples of adjectives from the Czech Subjectivity Lexicon, with the category/-ies to which it is assigned in the UCREL taxonomy. Each category is assigned a code consisting of a capital letter and a number,[45] with or without subnumbers. In addition, special characters are used, such as a + or − 'to indicate a positive or negative position on a semantic scale', and % or @ sign to mark rarity (see the whole list in Archer et al. 2002: 1–2). As shown in Table 8, many adjectives are assigned to multiple categories in that system, complicating the analysis. The columns 1–11 are ordered by the 'most likely tag first' as described in Archer et al. (2002: 1).[46] They thus indicate more likely to less likely semantic properties of the same adjective. For example, the adjectives *těžký* 'heavy, serious' and *tvrdý* 'hard, stiff' both belong to the category S1.2.5+ (*Toughness; strong*) and O4.1 (*General appearance and physical properties*). However, *těžký* is more likely to be semantically in group S1 than O4, whereas for *tvrdý* the opposite is true. Some more specific adjectives, such as *pochybný* 'dubious, questionable' and *odrazující* 'discouraging' only belong to one category each.[47]

---

[43] The annotation was only performed by the author.

[44] The full tagset can be viewed here: https://ucrel.lancs.ac.uk/usas/USASSemanticTagset.pdf.

[45] A full guide to which categories the letters and numbers refer to is available in Archer et al. (2002).

[46] The full list of translations can be found at https://github.com/UCREL/Multilingual-USAS/tree/master/Czech. [Accessed 26 March 2024].

[47] The translations into English are not included in Table 8, since they are not of importance as a categorisation example. Please see Figures 14 and 15, as well as Archer et al. (2002).

Table 8 Semantic categorisation of example adjectives, following the codes in Archer et al. (2002).

adjective	Semantic categories										
	1	**2**	**3**	**4**	**5**	**6**	**7**	**8**	**9**	**10**	**11**
těžký	N3.5+	S1.2.5+	N5+	O4.1	E4.1–	W4	A12–	A1.1.1	N3.2+	A1.1.2@	–
pochybný	A7–	–	–	–	–	–	–	–	–	–	–
tvrdý	O4.5	A12–	S1.2.5+	O4.1	–	–	–	–	–	–	–
odrazující	E4.1–	–	–	–	–	–	–	–	–	–	–
špatný	A5.1–	G2.2–	O4.2–	B2–	–	–	–	–	–	–	–

To tackle the issue of multiple categorisations from above, only the categories listed in column 1 were considered in this section, as it is stated to include the most likely meaning for those with multiple categorisations. Figures 14 and 15 reveal the most frequent categories for each year. Excluding multifunctional adjectives such as *velký* 'big, large', *dobrý* 'good', *poslední* 'last', and *rád* 'glad' allows for a clearer understanding of the adjectives that make a difference.

In Figure 14, five categorisations for the feminine co-occurrences remain consistent over time, with two consistently dominating.

In Figure 15, the decline for the masculine co-occurrences is consistent with Figure 13; men are evaluated less and less over time, and therefore appear less frequently in the dataset.

The following groups overlap, but the first is also the most prominent group of adjectives for women and the second for men here:

O4.2 Judgement of appearance (pretty etc.) most frequently co-occurs with the feminine nouns – mainly based on *krásný* 'beautiful' with *příjemný* 'nice, likeable'[48] and *hezký* 'nice, pretty', but also on *nemocný* 'sick, sickly' (which may be an appearance), *špatný* 'bad' and *zlý* 'mean, evil' being very prominent. This trend is less prominent with masculine adjectives, and these only appear in the later years, from 2005 onwards.

A5.1 Evaluation: good/bad competes for first place with the masculine, and is the second most prominent category for the feminine adjectives. The feminine adjectives include *trpící* 'suffering' and *mistrovský* 'masterly' together with, to a lesser extent, *civilizovaný* 'civil', *oslabený* 'weakened, short-handed' and *optimistický* 'optimistic'. With the masculine nouns, some very frequent adjectives are *špatný* 'bad', *silný* 'strong' and *nízký* 'low, short' (used to describe short men, workers with lower education, or lower-ranking employees). At the same time, *výborný* 'excellent' and *špičkový* 'top-notch' more frequently co-occur with nouns indicating men than women.

E4.1 Happy/sad is more prominent with women than men, although it comes up to top three for the men in 2003–2014. The driving force for the feminine there is *těžký* 'heavy, serious' being categorised in this group. Other prominent adjectives in this group include the more obvious *smutný* 'sad' and *šťastný* 'happy', but also *zoufalý* 'desperate, depressed'. Together, these contribute to strengthening the argument about women being evaluated more than men. For men, the adjectives include *těžký* 'heavy, serious' and (again) *nízký* 'low'.

---

[48] A reminder: the category used in this study is the one primarily noted as used with this meaning. It may have many more semantic categories.

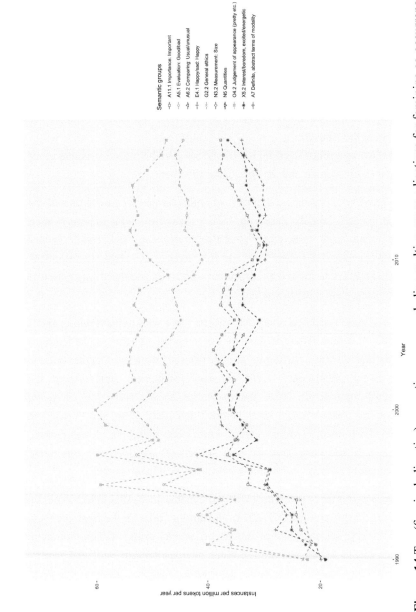

Figure 14 Top (five including ties) semantic groups, excluding multi-purpose adjectives for feminine co-occurrences.

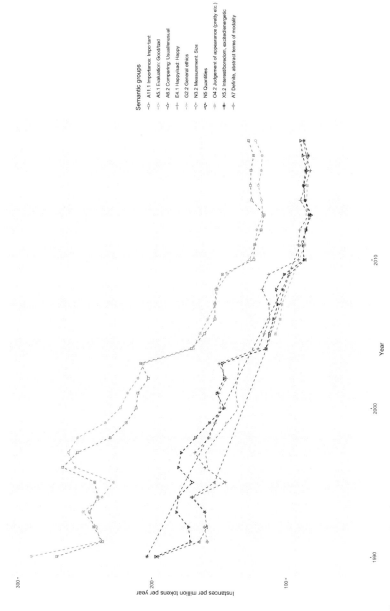

Figure 15 Top (five including ties) semantic groups, excluding multi-purpose adjectives, for masculine co-occurrences.

Additionally, *bohatý* 'rich, wealthy' is more commonly used to describe men than women.

N5 Quantities is more prominent among the masculine co-occurrences, derived from adjectives such as *těžký* 'heavy, serious' (again), but also *silný* 'strong' and *skvělý* 'excellent, great'.

A11.1 Importance: important competes with *A5.1 Evaluation: good/bad* for the most prominent category for the masculine adjectives here. For men, this category is mainly influenced by *důležitý* and *významný*, both of which can be translated as 'important', but the latter also 'relevant'. *Významný* 'relevant' is also a constant for female adjectives, but in third or fourth place, depending on the year.

Some groups appear and disappear, such as *G2.2 General ethics* over time. For example, for the 1990s the feminine dataset includes *svatý* 'holy' and *vystavený* 'exposed (to)' or 'displayed' – a glance in the corpus indicates that they are mainly present in the literary supplement to the morning paper *Lidové noviny* that had a monthly circulation of around 80,000 copies during this decade.[49] Again, the corpus was rather small in those years, hence the average value here gives even low frequencies a higher prominence than in later years. In 2004 and 2005, the adjective *stereotypní* 'stereotypical' boosts the semantic category *A6.2 Comparing: usual/unusual* as shown in Figure 14. It is important to note that even if adjectives co-occur with nouns, they may be far apart and only provide associations rather than actual collocations. For these semantic analyses, the distance between noun and adjective is weighed into the calculations, as in the subjectivity analyses in Section 3.3.2.

Compared with Coffey-Glover's (2019) table of semantic categorisation of masculine adjectives in women's magazines from 2008 (112), the category 'important' is consistent with this Czech data. Her top findings – 'shy' and 'romantic' in the first place, and 'dark' and 'stocky' in second – are, on the other hand, not all present in my data, due to the short Subjectivity Lexicon: *plachý* 'shy' is there, but with less than 0.05 per cent of the total amount of adjectives for men (and just above 0.05 for women) during most years.

The overall conclusions from this calculation of frequency of each semantic group are that the categories denoting judgement of appearance, happy/sad and evaluation of good/bad are more prominent with feminine nouns, while

---

[49] Numbers kindly provided by Petr Bednařík and Irena Reifová of the Department of Media Studies at Charles University, taken from old, printed documents without certain sources in their archives.

adjectives modifying masculine nouns more often co-occur with adjectives denoting excellence and strength. The main category found both in previous research and here is 'important', which also in these data mainly co-occur with the masculine nouns.

3.3.4 Adjectives and Noun as Co-Occurrences

This section focuses on the individual adjectives co-occurring with the two genders of this section (see Section 1.3). The adjectives that most likely modify the nouns, namely those that co-occur within one word of the noun, will be examined first. This overview is comprehensible when comparing only two groups, whereas it would be overwhelming in Section 2 on occupations.

Firstly, the adjectives co-occurring with nouns referring to women will be discussed. Figure 16 shows the quantitative data for the whole period: the top five adjectives per year (no negated forms were as frequent), apart from the multifunctional ones (see Section 3.2). For all years, the adjective that defines women in this dataset is *krásný* 'beautiful'. Every year, except for the first year when it only occurred on four occasions out of 239, this adjective is the most frequently used one to represent women in this dataset.

In Figure 16, 'beautiful' first reaches a peak in 1992, and remains the most frequent adjective from 1997 to 2018, except for 1996 when it is overtaken by *sociální* 'social'. This latter adjective is the second most frequent one over the years, as it can modify a variety of nouns, including 'democrat', 'worker' or even 'prostitute' (*sociální pracovnice* is a worker in both senses, although the latter meaning seems not to occur in the news). Additionally, the term appears in *ministryně sociálních věcí* 'female minister of social affairs'. During the first years, the term was mainly used to refer to social workers, which may be a remnant of news values from the previous regime.

Only two adjectives remain constant throughout the period: *zlý* 'bad, mean' during the first years, although not present in the top list of adjectives used during these years. This adjective is almost exclusively used with the nouns *žena* 'woman' and *čarodějnice* 'witch' but also with *sestra* 'sister' during 2011–2013. Upon examination, the vast majority of co-occurrences over time are either related to the Shakespearean play *Taming of the Shrew*, which in Czech is *Zkrocení zlé ženy*, or to a book entitled *Zlá žena* 'Evil Woman'. It does, however, also appear in sentences like *Protože moudrá žena, která umí s mužem zacházet, dosáhne mnohem více než žena zlá a hysterická* 'Because a wise woman, who

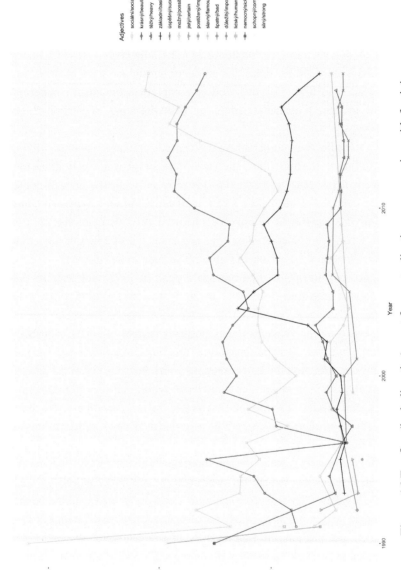

Figure 16 Top five (including ties) most frequent adjectives co-occurring with feminine nouns, per cent of female adjectives in the dataset per year.

knows how to handle a man, achieves much more than a mean and hysterical woman.'[50] The co-occurrence of *zlý* with *sestra* 'sister' or 'nurse' is partly due to a comparison with the Cinderella fairy tale that a lawyer made about the new constitution[51] and partly due to a new play with two 'evil sisters'.[52] The final constant is *zraněný* 'hurt, injured'. It is primarily used with the noun *žena* 'woman' but can also modify *důchodkyně* 'female pensioner' and co-occurs in the vicinity of hospital nouns such as *lékařka* 'female physician' and *sestra* 'nurse'. In other words, the adjective *zlý*, though frequent, rarely has the function of evaluating real-life women in the news, and *zraněný* often, but not always, occurs around female nouns of the caring professions handling hurt people. This serves as an example of the importance of handling large amounts of language data with care when drawing conclusions.

The discussion of individual adjectives is now reiterated, with the focus on those that co-occur with nouns referring to men. Figure 17 shows the diachronic frequencies.

Many adjectives take turns to compete for a top three ranking annually. A consistently high-ranking adjective is *zraněný* 'hurt, injured' that appears in 1994. (It is worth noting that there were officially no criminals running around hurting people during the previous regime; see e.g. Štanzel 2012:140). This term remains in the top three until 2018 and is mainly used to modify the nouns *muž* 'man' and *mladík* 'young man' followed by *voják* 'soldier' and *policista* 'police officer'.

The second most frequent adjective of the period is the increasingly used *bohatý*, 'rich'. This takes an extraordinary journey throughout the period from its debut in 1997 mainly referring to rich Americans and Russians but also Germans, Czechs and Jews (often in the context of either antisemitism or World War II). Despite a dip in 2009, the year after the European economic crisis of that decade, it peaks in 2014 and stays the most frequent adjective even after it has declined. In 2014, the nouns modified by *bohatý* are much more diverse than in 1997, and includes Ukrainians, Chinese, Indians, Jews, aristocrats and noblemen. From Section 3.3.1 it is clear that the semantic noun category REL contains a very small proportion of the nouns, but the use of *bohatý* significantly elevates

---

[50] *Nedělní Blesk* no. 7, 2016, corpus sentence ID: blne1607:18:48:4.

[51] *Hlavní autor nového občanského zákoníku / ... / jednou vysvětloval, jak ho trápí „problém Popelky". Totiž slabšího dědice, kterého ostatní („zlé sestry") přimějí, aby se vzdal svého nároku.* 'The main author of the new Civil Code / ... / once explained how he was troubled by the 'Cinderella problem'. That is, (the problem of) the weaker heir, whom the others ("the evil sisters") will force to give up her/his claim.' *Lidové Noviny* 11 November 2011, corpus sentence ID ln111111:35:4:2.

[52] *Dá se říct, že inscenace bude surrealistickou sondou do duše „zlé sestry".* 'You could say that the production will be a surreal probe into the soul of the "evil sister."' *Mladá fronta DNES* 1 March 2012, corpus sentence ID: mf120301:111:4:3.

Figure 17 Top five (including ties) most frequent adjectives co-occurring with masculine nouns, per cent of male adjectives in the dataset per year.

the visibility of one noun (Jew) within this category. Related to 'rich' is *slavný* 'famous', which appeared within the top three rankings in 1999 with intermittent appearances until 2014, subsequently settling into third place. This often goes together with *umělec* 'artist' (see also Section 2.5.2 on the occupational group Craft and Related Trades), *muž* 'man' and *bratr* 'brother', and slightly less often with Americans, Czechs and a few other nationalities. Of the occupational titles, *vědec* 'researcher' is the most prominent of the modified nouns.

Another of the more constant, recurring adjectives, albeit not in the top three every year, is *stínový* 'shadow', mainly used about shadow ministers (of the parliament) or shadow city mayors. See also the introduction to Section 3 on the shadow government of women in 2000.

This study of individual adjectives shows that the adjectives co-occurring with nouns referring to women and men in the corpus exhibit distinct patterns. The adjective *krásný* 'beautiful' is the most frequently used to describe women. In contrast, the adjectives co-occurring with nouns referring to men are more varied, with *zraněný* 'hurt, injured' and *bohatý* 'rich' being consistently high-ranking and *slavný* 'famous' also appearing intermittently. Furthermore, the study emphasises the significance of contextual considerations in the use of adjectives, as evidenced by the co-occurrence of *zlý* 'bad, mean' with the noun *žena* 'woman'. This co-occurrence is largely attributable to references to the Shakespearean play *Taming of the Shrew*.

3.4 Summary of the Representation of Gendered Nouns

The results of this section demonstrate that there is a clear difference in how women and men are represented: the high positivity for women is driven by the frequent use of the modifying adjectives for appearance, whereas men are positively represented by richness and competence. In a sense, de Beauvoir's (2011 [1949]) argument that men are positively represented may have been contradicted; if women would prefer to be seen as competent, then her theory holds also for these data, but if women would indeed prefer to be seen as beautiful and pleasant in their relations with others, then her theory is contra-dicted. However, Caldas-Caldas-Coulthard and Moon's (2010) observation about how the evaluation of women and men is asymmetrical, is upheld. At the same time, from a bird's-eye view, this comparison of two genders shows a comparatively balanced positive and negative evaluation, according to the Subjectivity Lexicon, compared to the previous sections on nationalities and occupations.

The evaluated co-occurrences are generally more frequent for women than men, which may mean that men are indeed the norm and do not get as evaluated in the news (see Figure 9). The analyses in Section 3.3.3 (Figures 14–15) seem to show that sickness, despair and desperation are rather frequent in relation to women. This is something that was not mentioned in previous research on similar data, but that seems to be a steady undercurrent in the data of this study based on the analyses of semantic categories and especially of the later years in newspapers. The noun *žena* 'woman' is also modified by *zlý* 'evil, bad', which can be blamed on Shakespeare and his fellow authors. The noun *sestra* 'sister' normally means a nurse, but often not when occurring with that particular adjective. Even if it does belong to the play title *Taming of the Shrew*, I argue it still contributes to the general (negative) picture of women outside of their occupational role. On the other hand, and just as in previous research, men are more likely to be associated with material happiness and less likely to be associated with emotions, based on the semantic categories. In terms of positivity and negativity, the clearest distinction for two equivalent nouns is that sisters are often evil[53] and brothers are often famous.

The evaluative female co-occurrences show a fluctuating trend. From 1990 to 2003, negativity decreased, but then increased, albeit to a lesser extent, between 2004 and 2018. Furthermore, positive evaluations experienced a decline from 2010 to 2018, particularly in the use of positively classified adjectives such as 'interesting', 'excellent' or 'happy' when describing women. Determining whether Cvrček's (2022) claim about a decreasing conformity in language styles of newspapers contributes to this phenomenon is challenging, but it should not be disregarded. A future study of different sources would reveal more about the differences caused by corpus composition and those caused by a consistently more negative discourse.

Despite all the masculine nouns in this dataset being the equivalents of the feminine nouns, there is clear androcentrism in the data (see Figures 13–15), similar to previous research. This must be seen in the morphological perspective of grammatical gender, where masculine forms are the norm not only in Slavonic, but also in many other Indo-European languages. However, it does not change the fact that female readers do not often encounter word forms where they are explicitly included.

4 Conclusions and Discussion

In this Element, the sections examine the representation of different social actors in the light of global statements from authorities such as the United Nations and the European Union that equality is a fundamental necessity for a prosperous society. The sections concern inequalities through linguistic othering and stratification in the Czech news during the thirty years after the democratic Velvet Revolution of

---

[53] This modifier, *zlý*, mainly occurs with *sestra* in the meaning of 'sister', not 'nurse'.

1989. Joining new calculations of previous studies on nationalities (Section 1.4), the sections on occupations (Section 2) and gender (Section 3) form an intersectional study on modern Czech printed news. Similarly to studies on other European languages, Czech news seems to reflect the idea that European and North American white-collar men are the norm and that other origins, as well as women and blue-collar occupations, are represented as deviating from that norm.

From a bird's-eye perspective, the adjectives from the Subjectivity Lexicon for Czech seem to give a clear stratification of nouns for nationalities and occupations. The lower the average income nationwide and the less supervisory functions at work, the fewer and more negative representations these nouns receive in the news. In contrast, the main result of the gender section is that nouns for women are more often represented by evaluative adjectives than those for men. It also shows that the slightly dominant positivity for these female nouns is based on appearance and emotions, whereas the masculine nouns are evaluated by importance and competence. At the same time, this bird's-eye perspective only performs well with these kinds of non-comprehensive sentiment tools when a discourse is overwhelming, as in the case of 'competent managers', 'beautiful women' or 'terrorist(-prone) Afghans'.

The advantages of utilising a bird's-eye view, a perspective of the whole data, are twofold. Firstly, the calculations of frequencies and dispersions are relatively quick. Secondly, the graphs produced indicate both the locations of peculiarities (high peaks or low troughs) and the existence of constant trends. As an alternative to an intuitive sampling of certain years, it is possible to discern particular occurrences, and then to pursue a more detailed examination of the relevant text around these occurrences. In this Element, the quantitative aspects are, as often as possible, accompanied by a closer study of the actual discourse. Due to the particular categorisations in the Subjectivity Lexicon, some parts that at first appeared very negative or positive were, in fact, more nuanced. Without a qualitative analysis and close reading, these nuances would have remained undetected. This is standard practice in corpus-assisted discourse studies and is essential to ensure accurate results. Furthermore, these overall calculations and graphs may provide a basis for further studies that extend beyond the domain of linguistics. Such studies may employ a range of methods, including close reading, interviews and surveys.

Close reading of the co-occurrence context reveals that most groups are driven by a few prominent nouns. These nouns cause more bias in Section 2 on the occupations, since their heterogeneity makes it difficult to make generalisations about the groups in that section as a whole. The details reveal that managers and physicians are the most frequently mentioned occupations, as are sports trainers. In terms of occupations, evaluated nouns for women include teachers, cleaners and models, whereas men have a much wider representation.

A close reading of the adjectives shows that female managers are more often represented by the adjective *schopný* 'competent' compared to the other female occupational nouns. A close reading of the discourse here reveals that in about half of the occurrences, female referents receive this modifier solely on the basis of their gender, whereas the men are regarded as inherently competent.

More importantly, the clearest out-groups are revealed by the relative frequency figures in combination with the qualitative reading from the previous studies. For the nationalities it is the low-income nationalities, Afghans in particular post-2000. For the occupations, specific groups such as clerks and soldiers (of both grammatical genders) are seen in both lesser numbers and a more negative light. There are small fluctuations during the most recent decades for the two genders, but it seems clear that women in the Czech news are still not nearly as much the norm as are the men. It also seems that despite there having been a constitution based on equality, 40 years of totalitarian communism and the more recent democratic system, none of these factors have assisted in creating an equal society.

This Element has contributed to research methodology on and in sentiment or subjectivity analysis through a language other than the ones most commonly studied. It also confirms that a well-executed list or lexicon is an excellent way to initiate a sentiment investigation. One reason for this is that it provides transparency. It took several years of effort from multiple researchers to compile the Subjective Lexicon for Czech, although it still requires further specific adjustments by others, and it must not constitute the only mode of analysis.

Regarding the aim of analysing equality, this Element indicates a lack of equality and equity in news texts in this less commonly studied language. Although there is a comparative balance between men and women, a closer examination reveals significant gender differences. There are strong imbalances in terms of how occupations and nationalities are represented, and this discrepancy suggests that statements on equality and equity found in international documents such as the Universal Declaration of Human Rights are not reflected in printed news texts. The sections show that although certain events can have a short-term impact on positive or negative representation, there is a consistent lack of equal representation in the Czech news press.

References

Alhamdan, B., Al-Saadi, K., Baroutsis, A., Du Plessis, A., Hamid, O. M. and Honan, E. (2014) Media Representation of Teachers across Five Countries. *Comparative Education*, 50(4), 490–505.

Archer, D., Wilson, A. and Rayson, P. (2002) *Introduction to the USAS Category System: Benedict project report*. Available at https://ucrel.lancs .ac.uk/usas/usas_guide.pdf. [Accessed: 1 October 2024].

Asgari, E. (2019) Life Language Processing: Deep Learning-Based Language-Agnostic Processing of Proteomics, Genomics/Metagenomics, and Human Languages. Doctoral dissertation. University of California, Berkeley.

Baker, P. (2014) *Using corpora to analyze gender*. London: Bloomsbury Academic.

Barát, E. (2005) The 'Terrorist Feminist': Strategies of Gate-Keeping in the Hungarian Printed Media. In Lazar, M. M. (ed.), *Feminist critical discourse analysis*. London: Palgrave Macmillan UK, pp. 205–228. [Online]. www .researchgate.net/publication/304735079_The_'Terrorist_Feminist'_Strategies_ of_Gate-Keeping_in_the_Hungarian_Printed_Media. DOI: https://doi.org/ 10.1057/9780230599901_9.

Benamara, F., Taboada M. and Mathieu, Y. (2017) Evaluative Language Beyond Bags of Words: Linguistic Insights and Computational Applications. *Computational Linguistics*, 43(1), 201–264.

Berrocal, M. (2017) Proximizing the Ukraine Conflict: The Case of the United States and the Czech Republic. *Lodz Papers in Pragmatics*, 13(2), 327–346. www.degruyter.com/document/doi/10.1515/lpp-2017-0016/html.

Bestvater, S. E. & Monroe, B. L. (2023) Sentiment Is Not Stance: Target-Aware Opinion Classification for Political Text Analysis. *Political Analysis*, 31(2), 235–256.

Birjali, M., Kasri, M. and Beni-Hssane, A. (2021) A Comprehensive Survey on Sentiment Analysis: Approaches, Challenges and Trends. *Knowledge-Based Systems*, 226, 107134.

Brookes, G. & McEnery, T. (2019) The Utility of Topic Modelling for Discourse Studies: A Critical Evaluation. *Discourse Studies*, 21(1), 3–21.

Caldas-Coulthard, C. R. & Moon, R. (2010) 'Curvy, Hunky, Kinky': Using Corpora as Tools for Critical Analysis. *Discourse & Society*, 21(2), 99–133.

Černá, Z. & Čech, R. (2019) Analysis of the Lemma Mateřství (Motherhood). *Jazykovedný časopis*, 70(2), 244–253.

Čmejrková, S. (2003) Czech: Communicating Gender in Czech. In Hellinger, M. & Bußmann, H. (eds.), *Gender across languages: The linguistic representation of women and men.* IMPACT: Studies in Language and Society 11, Vol. III. Amsterdam: John Benjamins Publishing Company. [Online]. https://benjamins.com/catalog/impact.11.06cme. DOI: https://doi.org/10.1075/impact.11.06cme.

Coffey-Glover, L. (2019) *Men in women's worlds: Constructions of masculinity in women's magazines.* London: Palgrave Macmillan UK. [Online]. https://link.springer.com/book/10.1057/978-1-137-57555-5. DOI: https://doi.org/10.1057/978-1-137-57555-5.

Cvrček, V. (2014) Proximita slov a možnosti jejího měření. In Nakladatelství Lidové Noviny/Ústav českého národní korpusu, *Kvantitativní analýza kontextu.* Studie z korpusové lingvistiky 18. Praha: Nakladatelství Lidové Noviny/Ústav českého národní korpusu.

Cvrček, V. (2022) Proměny registrů české žurnalistiky 1995–2018. *Časopis pro moderní filologii,* 104(1), 7–34. DOI: https://doi.org/10.14712/23366591.2022.1.1.

Cvrček, V., Laubeová, Z., Lukeš, D., Poukarová, P., Řehořková, A. and Zasina, A. J. (2020) *Registry v češtině (Registers in Czech).* Praha: Nakladatelství Lidové Noviny/Ústav českého národní korpusu.

Czech Statistical Office (2019) *Cizinci v ČR podle státního občanství v letech 1994–2018 (Foreigners in the CR by citizenship in the years 1994–2018 (as of 31 December)).* Available at https://csu.gov.cz/foreigners. [Accessed: 14 January 2024].

Czech Statistical Office (2020) *Labour market in the Czech Republic – time series: 1993–2019.* Available at https://bit.ly/3YEmBGU. [Accessed: 21 February 2023].

Delobelle, P. & Berendt, B. (2023) FairDistillation: Mitigating Stereotyping in Language Models. In Amini, M.-R., Canu, S., Fischer, A., Guns, T., Kralj Novak, P. and Tsoumakas, G. (eds.), *Machine learning and knowledge discovery in databases.* Lecture Notes in Computer Science, 13714. Cham: Springer International Publishing, pp. 638–654. [Online]. https://link.springer.com/chapter/10.1007/978-3-031-26390-3_37#citeas. DOI: https://doi.org/10.1007/978-3-031-26390-3_37.

Elmerot, I. (2017) These Women's Verbs: A Combined Corpus and Discourse Analysis on Reporting Verbs about Women and Men in Czech Media 1989–2015. Master's dissertation. Stockholm: Stockholm University. Available at https://urn.kb.se/resolve?urn=urn:nbn:se:su:diva-149414. [Accessed: 1 October 2024].

Elmerot, I. (2021) Income, Nationality and Subjectivity in Media Text. *Jazykovedný časopis/Journal of Linguistics*, 72(2), 667–678.

Elmerot, I. (2022) Constructing 'Us and Them' through Conflicts: Muslims and Arabs in the News 1990–2018. Pages 122–136 in Filardo-Llamas, L., Morales López, E. and Floyd, A. (eds.), *Discursive approaches to socio-political polarization and conflict*. Routledge Research in Language and Communication, 11. New York: Routledge. DOI: https://doi.org/10.4324/9781003094005-8.

Erikson, R., Goldthorpe, J. H. and Portocarero, L. (1979) Intergenerational Class Mobility in Three Western European Societies: England, France and Sweden. *The British Journal of Sociology*, 30(4), 415–441.

Erikson, R. & Goldthorpe, J. H. (1992) *The constant flux: A study of class mobility in industrial societies*. Oxford: Clarendon.

European Commission: Directorate General for Research and Innovation. (2019) Future of Scholarly Publishing and Scholarly Communication: Report of the Expert Group to the European Commission. Luxembourg: EU Publications Office. Available at https://data.europa.eu/doi/10.2777/836532.

Fairclough, N. (2011) *Media discourse*. London: Bloomsbury Academic.

Fairclough, N. (2015) *Language and power*. 3rd ed. London: Routledge.

Feinberg, M. (2006a) Dumplings and Domesticity: Women, Collaboration, and Resistance in the Protectorate of Bohemia and Moravia. Chapter 5 in Wingfield, N. M. & Bucur, M. (eds.), *Gender and war in twentieth-century Eastern Europe*. Indiana-Michigan Series in Russian and East European Studies. Bloomington, IN: Indiana University Press.

Feinberg, M. (2006b) *Elusive equality: Gender, citizenship, and the limits of democracy in Czechoslovakia, 1918–1950*. Pittsburgh, PA: University of Pittsburgh Press. [Online]. www.jstor.org/stable/j.ctt7zw9pd. DOI: https://doi.org/10.2307/j.ctt7zw9pd.

Feinberg, M. (2022) The Promise of Gender Equality in Interwar Central-Eastern Europe. Pages 303–310 in Fábián, K., Johnson, J. E. and Lazda, M. I. (eds.), *The Routledge handbook of gender in Central-Eastern Europe and Eurasia*. Routledge International Handbooks. London: Routledge.

Ferguson-Cradler G. (2023) Narrative and Computational Text Analysis in Business and Economic History. *Scandinavian Economic History Review*, 71(2), 103–127. DOI: https://doi.org/10.1080/03585522.2021.1984299.

Fidler, M. (2016) The Others in the Czech Republic: Their Image and Their Languages. *International Journal of the Sociology of Language*, 238, 37–58.

Fidler, M. & Cvrček, V. (2017) Keymorph Analysis, or How Morphosyntax Informs Discourse. *Corpus Linguistics and Linguistic Theory*, 15(1), 39–70.

Fidler, M. & Cvrček, V. (2018) Going Beyond 'Aboutness': A Quantitative Analysis of Sputnik Czech Republic. Pages 195–225 in Fidler, M. &

Cvrček, V. (eds.), *Taming the Corpus: From inflection and lexis to interpretation*. Quantitative Methods in the Humanities and Social Sciences. New York: Springer International.

Figenschou, T. U., Eide, E. and Einervoll Nilsen, R. (2021) Investigations of a Journalistic Blind Spot: Class, Constructors, and Carers in Norwegian Media. *Nordicom Review*, 42(s3), 71–87.

Fojtová, S. (2016) Contested Feminism: The East/West Feminist Encounters in the 1990s. Pages 111–125 in Jusová, I. & Šiklová, J. (eds.), *Czech feminisms: Perspectives on gender in East Central Europe*. Bloomington, IN: Indiana University Press. [Online]. www.google.com/books/edition/Czech_Feminisms/fLH-DAAAQBAJ?hl=en&kptab=getbook. DOI: https://doi.org/10.2307/j.ctt2005w2f.

Frančíková, D. (2017) *Women as essential citizens in the Czech national movement: The making of the modern Czech community*. Lanham, MD: Lexington Books.

Gregor, M. & Mlejnková, P. (2021) Facing Disinformation: Narratives and Manipulative Techniques Deployed in the Czech Republic. *Politics in Central Europe*, 17(3), 541–564.

Hackett, C. & Grim, B. J. (2012) *The Global Religious Landscape*. Washington, DC: Pew Research Center's Forum on Religion & Public Life. Available at https://assets.pewresearch.org/wp-content/uploads/sites/11/2012/12/globalReligion-tables.pdf. [Accessed: 14 May 2020].

Havelková, B. (2017) *Gender equality in law: Uncovering the legacies of Czech State socialism*. Oxford: Hart Publishing.

Havelková, H. & Oates-Indruchová, L. (eds.) (2015) *The politics of gender culture under state socialism: An expropriated voice*. London: Routledge.

Hedin, T. (2007) Gender and Language in Czech Talk Shows. In Bardel, C. & Erman, B. (eds.), *Language and gender from linguistic and textual perspectives*. Stockholm Studies in Modern Philology, 14, 17–36. Stockholm: Almqvist & Wiksell International.

Hodel, L., Formanowicz, M., Sczesny, S., Valdrová, J. and Von Stockhausen, L. (2017) Gender-Fair Language in Job Advertisements: A Cross-Linguistic and Cross-Cultural Analysis. *Journal of Cross-Cultural Psychology*, 48(3), 384–401.

Hoey, M. (2005) *Lexical priming: a new theory of words and language*. London: Routledge.

Ibroscheva, E. & Raicheva-Stover, M. (2009) Engendering Transition: Portrayals of Female Politicians in the Bulgarian Press. *Howard Journal of Communications*, 20(2), 111–128.

International Labour Organization (2004) *What is an occupational classification?* Available at www.ilo.org/public/english/bureau/stat/isco/docs/intro1.htm. [Accessed: 28 September 2020].

International Labour Organization (2008) *The International Standard Classification of Occupations – ISCO-08.* Available at https://isco.ilo.org/en/isco-08/. [Accessed: 21 November 2022].

International Labour Organization (2022) *International Standard Classification of Occupations (ISCO).* Available at https://isco.ilo.org/en/. [Accessed: 13 November 2022].

Islentyeva, A. (2018) The Undesirable Migrant in the British Press: Creating Bias through Language. *Neuphilologische Mitteilungen*, 119(2), 419–442. Helsinki: The Modern Language Society of Helsinki.

Jakobson, R. (1960) Closing Statement: Linguistics and Poetics. Pages 350–377 in Sebeok, T. A. (ed.), *Style in language.* Cambridge, MA: MIT Press.

Janda, L. A. & Clancy, S. J. (2006) *The case book for Czech.* Bloomington, IN: Slavica.

Jusová, I. (2016) Situating Czech Identity: Postcolonial Theory and 'the European Dividend'. Pages 29–45 in Jusová, I. & Šiklová, J. (eds.), *Czech feminisms: Perspectives on gender in East Central Europe.* Bloomington, IN: Indiana University Press. [Online]. https://vdoc.pub/download/czech-feminisms-perspectives-on-gender-in-east-central-europe-autbquu814q0. DOI: https://doi.org/10.2307/j.ctt2005w2f.5.

Kadlecová, K. (2010) *Ideologická perspektiva na stránkách ženských exkluzivních časopisů* [*Perspectives on ideology in women's magazines*]. [Online]. Available at https://dspace.cuni.cz/handle/20.500.11956/34946. Praha: Univerzita Karlova, Fakulta sociálních věd, Katedra mediálních studií.

Kanouse, D. E. & Hanson, L. R. (1972) Negativity in Evaluations. In Jones, E. E., Kanouse, D. E., Kelley, H. H., Nisbett, R. E., Valins, S. and Weiner, B. (eds.), *Attribution: Perceiving the causes of behavior*, pp. 47–62. Morristown, NJ: General Learning Press.

Katrňák, T. (2012) Is Current Czech Society a Social Class-Based Society? The Validity of EGP and ESeC Class Schemes. *Sociológia – Slovak Sociological Review*, 44(6), 678–703.

Kelly, E. F. & Stone, P. J. (1975) *Computer recognition of English word senses.* Amsterdam: North-Holland.

Klégr, A. (2007) *Tezaurus jazyka českého: slovník českých slov a frází souznačných, blízkých a příbužných.* Praha: Nakladatelství Lidové noviny.

Knoblock, N. (ed.) (2020) *Language of conflict: Discourses of the Ukrainian crisis.* New York, NY: Bloomsbury Academic.

Křen, M. (2017). Grammatical Change Trends in Contemporary Czech Newspapers. *Journal of Linguistics/Jazykovedný Casopis*, 68(2), 238–248.

Kress, B. (2012) *Totalitarian political discourse? Tolerance and intolerance in Eastern and East Central European countries: Diachronic and synchronic aspects.* Frankfurt: Peter Lang.

Kubát M., Mačutek J. and Čech R. (2021) Communists spoke differently: An analysis of Czechoslovak and Czech annual presidential speeches. *Digital Scholarship in the Humanities*, 36(1), 138–152. https://doi.org/10.1093/llc/fqz089.

Lei, L. & Liu, D. (2021) *Conducting sentiment analysis*. Cambridge: Cambridge University Press. DOI: https://doi.org/10.1017/9781108909679.

Loughran, T. & McDonald, B. (2011) When Is a Liability Not a Liability? Textual Analysis, Dictionaries, and 10-Ks. *The Journal of Finance*, 66(1), 35–65.

Mahlberg M. (2005) *English general nouns: a corpus theoretical approach*. Amsterdam: John Benjamins.

Malík, R. & Pavlasová, H. (2018) Sentiment Analýza Médií: Mediální obraz druhé přímé prezidentské volby v ČR. *Medium*. Available at: https://medium.com/@radkamalik/mediální-obraz-druhé-přímé-prezidentské-volby-v-čr-míra-a-sentiment-medializace-jednotlivých-2910da7d3177. [Accessed: 8 May 2023].

McPherson M., Smith-Lovin L. and Cook J.M. (2001) Birds of a Feather: Homophily in Social Networks. *Annual Review of Sociology*, 27(1), 415–444. DOI: https://doi.org/10.1146/annurev.soc.27.1.415.

Moreno-Ortiz, A., Pérez-Hernández, C. and García-Gámez, M. (2022) The Language of Happiness in Self-Reported Descriptions of Happy Moments: Words, Concepts, and Entities. *Humanities and Social Sciences Communications*, 9(1), 181.

Musílek, K. & Katrňák, T. (2015) The Notion of Social Class in Czech Political Discourse. *Sociologický časopis*, 51(3), 387–416.

Nguyen, T. M. & Do, A. D. (2022) 'Second-Class Citizens': Framing Domestic Migrant Workers in Vietnamese News Media during the Fourth Wave of COVID-19. *Media Asia*, 1–20.

Nyklová, B. (2018) Gender Studies in the Czech Republic: Institutionalisation Meets Neo-liberalism Contingent on Geopolitics. In Kahlert, H. (ed.), *Gender studies and the new academic governance*, pp. 255–280. Wiesbaden: Springer Fachmedien Wiesbaden. DOI: https://doi.org/10.1007/978-3-658-19853-4_12.

Oates-Indruchová, L. (2016) Unraveling a Tradition, or Spinning a Myth? Gender Critique in Czech Society and Culture. *Slavic Review*, 75(4), 919–943.

Pantić, M. (2017) Adjectival Attributes with the Nouns 'čovek', 'žena', 'muškarac' and 'muž'. *Infotheca*, 17(2), 66–96.

Parlament Československé Republiky (1920) *121/1920 Sb. Ústava 1920* [*The Czechoslovak Constitution of 1920*]. Available at https://psp.cz/docs/texts/ constitution_1920.html. [Accessed: 19 March 2020].

Piao, S., Rayson, P., Archer, D., et al. (2016) Lexical Coverage Evaluation of Large-Scale Multilingual Semantic Lexicons for Twelve Languages. In *Proceedings of the Tenth International Conference on Language Resources and Evaluation (LREC 2016)*, pp. 2624–2619. Paris, France: European Language Resources Association (ELRA). Available at www.lrec-conf.org/ proceedings/lrec2016/summaries/257.html. [Accessed: 10 March 2022].

Rao, P. & Taboada, M. (2021) Gender Bias in the News: A Scalable Topic Modelling and Visualization Framework. *Frontiers in Artificial Intelligence*, 4, 664737.

Šklovskij, V. (1914 [1973]) The Resurrection of the Word. In Bann, S. & Bowlt, J. E. (eds.), *Russian formalism: A collection of articles and texts in translation*. Edinburgh: Scottish Academic Press. Available at www.scribd.com/ document/324530861/SHKLOVSKY-Viktor-The-Resurrection-of-the-Word.

Šonková, J. (2011) Genderové rozdíly v mluvené češtině [Gender differences in spoken Czech]. In Čermák, F., Hajičová, E. and Macurová, A. (eds.), *Výzkum a výstavba korpusů*. Korpusová lingvistika. Praha: NLN, Nakladatelství Lidové noviny Ústav Českého národního korpusu.

Štanzel, A. (2012) Ordnung und Sicherheit, Devianz und Kriminalität im Staatssozialismus. Die Tschechoslowakei und die DDR 1948/49–1989. *Bohemia*, 52(1), 140–146.

Stefanowitsch, A., & Middeke, K. (2023). Gender-Marking -ess: The Suffix that Failed. *Zeitschrift für Anglistik und Amerikanistik*, 71(3), 293–319.

Štětka, V. & Mihelj, S. (2024). *The Illiberal Public Sphere: Media in Polarized Societies*. Cham: Springer Nature. DOI: https://doi.org//10.1007/978-3-031-54489-7.

Stubbs, M. (2002) *Words and phrases: Corpus studies of lexical semantics*. Oxford: Blackwell Publishers.

Taboada, M., Brooke, J., Tofiloski, M., Voll, K. and Stede, M. (2011) Lexicon-Based Methods for Sentiment Analysis. *Computational Linguistics*, 37(2), 267–307.

Tahal, K. (2010) *A Grammar of Czech as a Foreign Language*. Prague: Factum CZ, s.r.o.

Thál, J. & Elmerot, I. (2022) Unseen Gender: Misgendering of Transgender Individuals in Czech. In Knoblock, N. (ed.), *The Grammar of Hate*. Cambridge: Cambridge University Press. DOI: https://doi.org/10.1017/ 9781108991841.006.

Tognini-Bonelli, E. (2001) *Corpus linguistics at work*. Amsterdam: John Benjamins Publishing Company.

Trčková, D. (2018) Newspaper Portrayal of Teachers: A Comparative Study of Representations of Teachers in a British and a Czech Broadsheet. *Discourse and Interaction*, 11(2), 87–103.

Tuček, M. (2019) *Prestiž povolání – červen 2019*. Praha: Centrum pro výzkum veřejného mínění, Sociologický ústav AV ČR, v.v.i. Available at https://cvvm.soc.cas.cz/media/com_form2content/documents/c2/a4986/f9/eu190724.pdf.

Ulfsdotter Eriksson, Y. & Nordlander, E. (2022) On the Discrepancy of Descriptive Facts and Normative Values in Perceptions of Occupational Prestige. *Sociological Research Online*, 28(3), 1–20. DOI: https://doi.org/10.1177/13607804221075357.

United Nations (n/a) 'Goal 5: Achieve Gender Equality and Empower All Women and Girls.' www.un.org/sustainabledevelopment/gender-equality/. [Accessed: 22 February 2024].

United Nations (1948) *Universal declaration of human rights*. United Nations. www.un.org/en/about-us/universal-declaration-of-human-rights. [Accessed: 13 August 2024].

van Dijk, T. A. (1988). *News as discourse*. Hillsdale, NJ: Lawrence Erlbaum Associates.

van Leeuwen, M. H. D., Maas, I. and Miles, A. (2002a) *HISCO: Historical international standard classification of occupations*. Leuven, Belgium: Leuven University Press.

van Leeuwen, M. H. D. (2002b) *HISCO tree of occupational groups*. Available at https://historyofwork.iisg.nl/major.php. [Accessed: 18 April 2023].

United Nations Statistics Division (2020) *Population by religion, sex and urban/rural residence 1996–2018 (Demographic Statistics Database)*. United Nations. Available at: https://data.un.org/Data.aspx?d=POP&f=tableCode%3a28. [Accessed: 1 October 2024].

Veselovská, K. (2017) *Sentiment analysis in Czech*. Prague: Ústav formální a aplikované lingvistiky [Institute of Formal and Applied Linguistics].

Veselovská, K. & Bojar, O. (2013) *Czech SubLex 1.0*. Available at https://lindat.mff.cuni.cz/repository/xmlui/handle/11858/00-097C-0000-0022-FF60-B. [Accessed: 1 October 2024].

Viola, L. (2023) *The humanities in the digital: Beyond critical digital humanities*. [Online]. https://link.springer.com/book/10.1007/978-3-031-16950-2. Cham: Springer International Publishing. DOI: http://doi.org/10.1007/978-3-031-16950-2.

Weiner, E. (2007) *Market dreams: Gender, class, and capitalism in the Czech Republic*. [Online]. Ann Arbor, MI: University of Michigan Press. DOI: http://doi.org/10.3998/mpub.206852.

Weiner, E. & MacRae, H. (2017) Opportunity and Setback? Gender Equality, Crisis and Change in the EU. In Kantola, J. & Lombardo, E. (eds.), *Gender and the Economic Crisis in Europe*. Gender and Politics Series. Cham: Springer International Publishing, pp. 73–93. DOI: http://doi.org/10.1007/978-3-319-50778-1_4.

Wilson T., Wiebe J. and Hoffmann P. (2005) Recognizing Contextual Polarity in Phrase-Level Sentiment Analysis. In *Proceedings of Human Language Technology Conference and Conference on Empirical Methods in Natural Language Processing*, Vol. H05-1. Vancouver, British Columbia, Canada: Association for Computational Linguistics, pp. 347–354. https://aclanthology.org/H05-1044

Wodak, R. (2016) What CDA is about: A Summary of Its History, Important Concepts and Its Developments. In R. Wodak & M. Meyer, eds., *Methods of critical discourse analysis*, 3rd ed. London: Sage Publications, pp. 1–13.

World Bank Group (2020) *World bank country and lending groups*. Available at https://datahelpdesk.worldbank.org/knowledgebase/articles/906519-world-bank-country-and-lending-groups. [Accessed: 16 April 2020].

Zasina, A. J. (2018) Image of politicians and gender in Czech daily newspapers. In Fidler, M. & Cvrček, V. (eds.), *Taming the corpus: From inflection and lexis to interpretation*. Quantitative methods in the humanities and social sciences, pp. 167–194. Cham: Springer International Publishing.

Zasina, A. J. (2019) Gender-Specific Adjectives in Czech Newspapers and Magazines. *Jazykovedný časopis*, 70(2), 299–312.

Zhang, B. H., Lemoine, B. and Mitchell, M. (2018) Mitigating Unwanted Biases with Adversarial Learning. In *AIES '18: Proceedings of the 2018 AAAI/ACM Conference on AI, Ethics, and Society*, pp. 335–340. Available at https://dl.acm.org/doi/10.1145/3278721.3278779. DOI: https://doi.org/10.1145/3278721.3278779.

Zhao M., and Schütze H. (2019) A Multilingual BPE Embedding Space for Universal Sentiment Lexicon Induction. In *Proceedings of the 57th Annual Meeting of the Association for Computational Linguistics*. Florence, Italy: Association for Computational Linguistics, pp. 3506–3517.

Ädel, A. (2020) Corpus Compilation. In Paquot, M. & Gries, S. Th. (eds.), *A practical handbook of corpus linguistics*. Cham: Springer International Publishing. DOI: https://doi.org/10.1007/978-3-030-46216-1_1.

Acknowledgements

This Element has been made open access in digital format by means from Stiftelsen Längmanska kulturfonden, as well as by the Humanities Faculty Club and the Profile area Language and Power at Stockholm University. The author would like to thank chief editor Susan Hunston for her thorough work to improve this Element, as well as professors Masako Ueda Fidler and Václav Cvrček for their input on Czech society, and Klas Rönnbäck for the idea of using not only ISCO but also the historical equivalent.

Cambridge Elements ☰

Corpus Linguistics

Susan Hunston

University of Birmingham

Professor of English Language at the University of Birmingham, UK. She has been involved in Corpus Linguistics for many years and has written extensively on corpora, discourse, and the lexis-grammar interface. She is probably best known as the author of *Corpora in Applied Linguistics* (2002, Cambridge University Press). Susan is currently co-editor, with Carol Chapelle, of the Cambridge Applied Linguistics series.

Advisory Board

Professor Paul Baker, *Lancaster University*
Professor Jesse Egbert, *Northern Arizona University*
Professor Gaetanelle Gilquin, *Université Catholique de Louvain*

About the Series

Corpus Linguistics has grown to become part of the mainstream of Linguistics and Applied Linguistics, as well as being used as an adjunct to other forms of discourse analysis in a variety of fields. It continues to become increasingly complex, both in terms of the methods it uses and in relation to the theoretical concepts it engages with. The Cambridge Elements in Corpus Linguistics series has been designed to meet the needs of both students and researchers who need to keep up with this changing field. The series includes introductions to the main topic areas by experts in the field as well as accounts of the latest ideas and developments by leading researchers.

Cambridge Elements ≡

Corpus Linguistics

Printed in the United States
by Baker & Taylor Publisher Services